Complete CardioKickboxing

Complete CardioKickboxing

A Safe & Effective Approach to High Performance Living

YMAA Publication Center
Boston, Mass. USA

YMAA Publication Center
Main Office:
    4354 Washington Street
    Boston, Massachusetts, 02131
    617-323-7215 • ymaa@aol.com • www.ymaa.com

10 9 8 7 6 5 4 3 2 1

Edited by Andrew Conry-Murray
Cover Design by Richard Rossiter

ISBN: 1-886969-80-9

Anatomy drawings copyright ©1994 by TechPool Studios Corp. USA, 1463 Warrensville
Center Road, Cleveland, OH 44121

Publisher's Cataloging in Publication
(Prepared by Quality Books Inc.)

Seabourne, Thomas.
    CardioKickboxing : a safe & effective approach to
high performance living / author, Tom Seabourne ;
editor, Andrew Murray. -- 1st ed.
    p. cm.
    ISBN: 1-886969-80-9

    1. Kickboxing. 2. Exercise. 3. Physical
fitness. I. Title.

GV1114.65.S43 2000   613.7'1
           QBI99-901224

Disclaimer:
The authors and publisher of this material are NOT RESPONSIBLE in any manner
whatsoever for any injury which may occur through reading or following the instructions
in this manual.
The activities, physical or otherwise, described in this material may be too strenuous or
dangerous for some people, and the reader(s) should consult a physician before engaging
in them.

Printed in Canada

Table of Contents

Foreword

In 1992, I created the original Cardio Kickboxing® workout program. The objective was the promote the *sport* of kickboxing through kickboxing for *fitness.* I have had over three decades of experience in the martial arts, twenty of which were spent as a trainer, manager, sanctioning body rep., TV commentator and promoter for the sport of American-style kickboxing, formerly known as full-contact karate. My agenda and mission was and has always been to safely mainstream the workout of a fighter to the general public for its fitness and self-defense benefits. Thus, our program has always focused on sport-specific techniques used in boxing, kickboxing, and Thai-style kickboxing. The program has also always been equipment intensive using conventional boxing and kickboxing training tools such as heavy bags, uppercut bags, double-end bags, punch mitts, focus pads, etc., which provide:

- A resistance component to an already demanding cardio vascular workout for greater fitness benefits, and
- Techniques that are authentic and efficient so that they could be effective for self-defense purposes.

In order to introduce this workout concept to the market, we approached a number of fitness video companies to produce a video for us, but there was no interest. Pioneers generally wind up with lots of arrows stuck in themselves. Consequently, we self-produced *Cardio Kickboxing, The Workout with a Kick!* video in 1993 as well as registered the name and trademark. I always believed this workout would be a hit. With a lot of hard work at the grassroots level sending out hundreds of press releases and complimentary preview copies of the video to various media sources, doing countless demos and interviews, we found that, seven years later, we were an overnight success.

Over time, the program has become an alternative to conventional aerobics, now called group fitness classes. Initially, the aerobics industry was not interested in working with us to help develop a certification program so, again, we developed our own having now certified hundreds of instructors here in the U.S. and overseas. The program is grounded in techniques from the sport of kickboxing as well as martial arts, not necessarily aerobics. Having worked in the fitness industry myself, I recognized the need for tailoring the program to meet the needs of those who were not necessarily as physically fit or as young as some of the competitive fighters I had worked with over the years. I also recognize that there are space and budget limitations in health clubs and martial arts schools so we also began offering a "without" equipment option for our instructors. However, they are still required to go through and pass the "with" equipment components first and are then allowed to dovetail off of the original program. With so many people having already been exposed to boxing, kickboxing and martial arts who might wind up in their classes, they had better know their stuff to maintain credibility and stay at least one step ahead of their students' learning curve.

Unlike some of my martial arts brethren who would never consider deviating from how they were taught by their instructor, we actually encourage our prospective instructors to bring their own personality and style of presentation into the mix based on their background and teaching experience. Otherwise, to do things my way would certainly stifle creativity. Instead of just mimicking the moves, we provide them with the biomechanically correct knowledge of how to throw a punch or kick as well as an understanding of the terminology, jargon, and history of how the program evolved from a sport into a fitness program. For example, understanding spatial relationships of an opponent is essential to understanding any martial art or kickboxing program. A kickboxer has only one opponent. Why would he need a back kick in his environment inside the ring? A martial artist might need one if he is surrounded by several attackers in the street, but a kickboxer has one opponent in front of him—no need for a back kick unless he intends to take out the referee. Learning these basic and fundamental concepts enable our instructors to be better prepared and more confident when teaching.

Even though I felt this workout concept would be a success, I never envisioned it would become as big as it has. Every so-called fitness guru or aerobics queen is now coming out of the woodwork with his or her own "kickboxing" video. Success breeds imitation. Cardio kickboxing has spawned many hybrid programs some of which are more aerobics rather than kickboxing oriented. I have actually had an aerobics instructor recently request a refund for the original Cardio kickboxing video because, she said, "it wasn't 'cardio kickboxing' (as she knew it)." How's that for being uniformed and arrogant?

There has been a recent tendency to water-down the program and make up movements that will fit neatly and tidily into an aerobics class format to conform to the beat of the music. This is not necessary with all the additional techniques available in kickboxing which we refer to as "add-ons" to the basics. The participants in these classes would be better served by their instructors not taking that approach. Otherwise, their program may go the way of the many products marketed through infomercials—in the hallway closet or garage sale. Lots of sizzle with little substance does not lend itself to longevity.

Even though the origins of our sport date back to the Shaolin Temple built in Henan Province in China in 495 A.D., I have found that many traditional martial artists lack an in depth knowledge of conditioning and safety that is of utmost priority demanded by the health and fitness industry. Conversely, the health and fitness industry which is really still in its infancy, by comparison, having come into its own only about thirty years ago, knows little about kickboxing. The goal of my company and of Dr. Tom Seabourne is to unite the two industries and thus the need for a comprehensive book on this subject.

Frank Thiboutot, President
Sport Karate, Inc.

Preface

Cardio Kickboxing® is the hottest trend in fitness. It combines martial arts, aerobics, and music for a dynamic and effective workout. Whether you're a martial artist or someone looking to add a little variety to your exercise program, this book has all the information and inspiration you need to improve your fitness.

Complete CardioKickboxing takes the guesswork out of your workouts. The drills in this book utilize all of your muscle groups, providing a non-impact, full-body workout to increase your cardiovascular endurance, strength, and power. You'll enjoy increased fitness and develop powerful punches, kicks, strikes, and blocks.

You can create a fitness regimen tailored to your needs with *Complete CardioKickboxing's* step-by-step program. You'll learn to modify your intensity and vary your workouts for peak performance. You can use this book to work out at home, or to complement what you learn in the many fitness clubs that offer cardio kickboxing classes. This variety and adaptability make cardio kickboxing inspiring. It is different from other fitness trends that come and go—cardio kickboxing keeps the body and mind excited.

This book explains how to punch, kick, strike, block, and throw combinations like a pro. If you've never tried cardio kickboxing before, this book will give you a foundation in the basics, and help you sharpen your cardio kickboxing skills. If you're an experienced cardio kickboxer, you'll discover both great exercises to enhance your skills and dynamic workouts to improve your speed, flexibility, and endurance.

Chapter 1 prepares you for your cardio kickboxing workout. It presents guidelines for motivation, and prepares you for a successful cardio kickboxing experience. This information leaves you ready and waiting to perform the basic punches, kicks, stances, combinations, and drills that are presented in Chapters 4 through 8.

A unique feature of *Complete CardioKickboxing* compared to other aerobic programs is the mind/body experience. Chapter 2, Mind and Body, discusses relaxation, focus, breathing, visualization, and goal setting. Chapter 3 describes correct posture and stretching techniques for cardio kickboxing.

Cardio kickboxing is the ultimate physical training routine. It is both aerobic and anaerobic, and it works every muscle group in your body. Chapters 9 and 10 teach you how to burn fat, build endurance and speed, and recover properly for optimum performance and safety.

Chapters 11 through 14 present a variety of drills and exercises, including home training, to help keep your workouts fun and interesting. Chapter 15 offers advice on what to look for in a good instructor, and how to make cardio kickboxing a lifelong pursuit.

After reading this book, you'll be able to create your own individualized program to meet your fitness needs and goals. You'll understand how to fulfill your potential, and you'll reach levels of confidence, power, quickness, and endurance you never thought possible.

Now let's get to it!

Acknowledgments

Thanks to my instructors in Okinawa and Korea who provided the basic techniques for me to make cardio kickboxing® into a workout extraordinaire. And thanks to my children Alaina, Grant, Laura, Susanna, and Julia who tried out all of my new combinations and routines before I took them public. And to my wife Danese, who kept refueling our muscle glycogen stores with nutrient-dense carbohydrates and proteins.

A special thanks to Andrew Conry-Murray who did a fantastic job of editing *Complete CardioKickboxing*, and to YMAA Publication Center for letting me share my ideas with you, the reader.

Introduction

Studies demonstrate that a key to exercise adherence is variety. Your cardio kickboxing® program is constantly evolving from beginner to expert. This diversity in your training develops ultimate fitness without overtraining. An overweight, compulsive jogger may save his or her knees by switching to cardio kickboxing.

Cardio kickboxing is different from other exercise programs. Form, breathing, and posture are emphasized. A warm-up, stretching, punching, and kicking drills, and a cooldown are all incorporated into a single cardio kickboxing workout.

A focused mind is just as important as a fit body. But you may find it too hard or time-consuming to meditate. You can combine cardio kickboxing with present-minded focus. Concentrate on your movements rather than your worries.

Slow down if your heart is racing. Monitor your breathing. If you are huffing and puffing, pace yourself. This is your workout. If you cannot keep up with the fast beat of the music, train to the slow beat. This is not a race. There is no finish line. It takes as long as it takes.

Getting Started

Why Cardio Kickboxing?

Cardio kickboxing® can get you into the best shape of your life. It's a terrific cardiovascular workout and great for muscular endurance. *Muscle and Fitness* magazine reported a study demonstrating that this type of exercise is a fantastic calorie burner; more so than basketball, running, or swimming.

Cardio kickboxing is different from karate or aerobics. It combines martial arts, aerobics, and music for a workout that never gets boring. It's also easy to learn. The step-by-step training provided in this book will give you the necessary tools to develop strength, flexibility, and endurance.

As you'll see in the pages of this book, there are dozens of punches, kicks, blocks, stances, and combinations that you can learn. This variety is one of the things that makes cardio kickboxing fun. There is always something new to learn, something to improve.

The versatile cardio kickboxing programs presented in this book are holistic, cross-training workouts. All of the exercises are natural and safe. They may be practiced in a studio or in the privacy of your home. Music and mirrors are helpful, but no additional equipment is necessary.

So whether your goal is a trimmer waistline, more energy, or improved self-confidence, cardio kickboxing will deliver.

Cardio Kickboxing and Self-Defense

Cardio kickboxing is popular because not only does it improve your cardiovascular conditioning and help you to lose body fat, it increases your self-confidence. Learning a variety of punches, kicks, strikes, and blocks helps you to feel more comfortable in case you are required to handle yourself in a self-defense situation. But keep in mind that *cardio kickboxing is a fitness activity, not a self-defense program*. Although you will learn martial arts techniques, they will not transform you into Jackie Chan. Do not confuse cardio kickboxing with self-defense training.

With that said, if you are truly inspired by cardio kickboxing, and you would like to hone your skills for self-defense or martial arts competition, there are martial arts studios in just about every city in the United States. The martial arts programs that are most similar to cardio kickboxing are Japanese karate, Korean taekwondo, Chinese kung fu, kickboxing, and muai thai.

If you have previously trained in the martial arts, you will find cardio kickboxing to be an exemplary cross-training activity to improve your martial arts performance. Simply adapt the cardio kickboxing strategies to your own techniques. For example, if your style of martial arts does not permit you to kick above the waist, keep all of your kicks low. Or, if you only twist your wrist a quarter turn on your punches rather than turning your palm towards the floor, do it your way. As long as all of your techniques are biomechanically correct and safe, so be it. Cardio kickboxing is a flexible and fun way to add some variety (and a great workout) to your regular martial arts training.

Environment

You can practice cardio kickboxing on level ground outdoors, in a traditional aerobics studio with a carpeted or wooden floor, or even in your hotel room. No equipment is necessary; however, you can use hand wraps, gloves, kicking pads, jump ropes, finger- free boxing gloves, and punching and kicking bags to increase the intensity of your workout and create a martial arts ambiance.

Guidelines

You've finally discovered the ultimate workout and you're no doubt anxious to start reaping the rewards. Visualize a strong, sleek body. See yourself having achieved your fitness goals.

Safety is my first concern as I place you on your road to peak fitness. So before you turn on your music and begin punching and kicking, take a few minutes to learn what you need for cardio kickboxing success.

Hydration. Your body is composed of about sixty-five percent water. It is imperative that you remain hydrated while cardio kickboxing. Drink one to two cups of fluid twenty minutes before you begin your workout so you are well-hydrated. Depending on the room temperature, you should easily finish sixteen ounces of water after a one-hour workout. If the room is hot, drink more because you will be perspiring at a much more rapid rate than normal. If you are pregnant, hypoglycemic, diabetic, or plan on cardio kickboxing longer than forty minutes, seek advice from your physician. Your physician may require you to sip a carbohydrate drink when cardio kickboxing to help keep up your blood sugar levels.

Nutrition. Cardio kickboxing burns significant calories. Compared to the average aerobic step class that burns between three hundred and four hundred calories per hour, cardio kickboxing burns between five hundred and eight hundred calories in that same one-hour period.

Fuel your muscles before and after your workout. Regardless of your weight loss goals, you should be sure that your muscle glycogen stores are full both before and after your training. Eat an energy bar, a banana, a fig bar or a cup of yogurt an hour or so before your workout, and be sure to eat regular, well-balanced meals throughout the day. Keep in mind that fat burns in a muscular furnace.

For more information on nutrition and exercise, my book *The Martial Arts Athlete* goes into great detail about a winning eating program.

Warming Up. Your warm-up is very important. Use this time to mentally prepare for cardio kickboxing.

Begin with a five- to eight-minute warm-up that uses a variety of easy punches and blocks. (You'll learn punching and blocking in Chapters 5 and 7, respectively.) Jabs, punches, and hooks are a good start to your program. You can double up on your jabs and hooks for variety. Be careful not to do a lot of shuffling and kicking during your warm-up. These movements are too vigorous. Instead, get your blood flowing with some easy punching drills, and mentally prepare for the remainder of your workout.

When warming up, execute your techniques slowly but with perfect form. Instead of throwing rapid-fire attacks and then resting, execute one perfect slow-motion block and strike. This is a great time to focus on your form and practice all the little details that go into a perfect punch.

Jumping rope, with or without a rope, is an excellent warm-up exercise. It improves your footwork and helps you prepare for cardio kickboxing. Vary the intensity by altering the types and number of jumps. You can skip, double-hop, or cross your arms. Use your wrists to turn the rope (or imaginary rope).

To jump properly, hold your hands at your waist about two inches from your body. Jump low. Spin the rope so it barely touches the floor. Skip lightly on the balls of your feet with your knees bent to take the strain off your shins. Beginners should try and jump three one-minute rounds with a thirty-second rest between each round. Increase your duration one minute per round every two weeks until you can comfortably jump three three-minute rounds.

Moving to the Beat

Cardio kickboxing to music is energizing! You'll enjoy performing your moves to the beat of your favorite tunes. Time passes quickly. Before you know it, you will have completed all of your punches, kicks, strikes, and blocks. Even if you don't think you have rhythm, give it a try. The beat keeps you moving.

At first, just think about the form of each technique and listen to the music in the background. After you feel comfortable with your moves, practice punching and kicking to the beat. Soon you will be combining punching and kicking combinations and working every muscle in your body.

In general, the faster you throw your punches and kicks, the more advanced your workout becomes. If you are a beginner, and have never tried cardio kickboxing, practice your moves slowly and with control. Focus mainly on your form.

Music Selection

Music selection for cardio kickboxing is very specific. Look for music with between 125 and 130 beats per minute. To figure out beats per minute, count the downbeats in a song for thirty seconds and multiply by two.

Some of my favorite songs to use in a workout include:

"The Music Is Movin," Brooklyn Bounce

"It Feels So Good," Sonique

"Enola-Gay," OMD

"Tomorrow," Arrola

"Carnival de Paris," Dario G.

"What's Up," DJ Miko

"African Dream," Soweto Funk

You can perform your cardio kickboxing techniques to the slow speed beat, the medium speed beat, or the fast speed beat. The slow beat is when you count two beats as you complete each punch or kick. At the medium beat, match each punch or kick to the beat of your music. The fast beat is punching and kicking double-time; that is, twice as fast as your medium beat.

After you practice your individual punches and kicks to the music, take two or three different kicks and/or punches and piece them together into combinations. This is advanced and should not be performed unless you have perfect form for all of your punches and kicks. Never sacrifice form for speed.

How to Get It Right

Practice cardio kickboxing regularly, whether daily or two to three times a week. If you decide to train every day, use different techniques. Practice your punches, kicks, strikes, and blocks at different speeds, heights, and angles. The key to success is steady, consistent practice.

It is not a great idea to perform multitudes of complicated, choreographed drills within each workout. Instead, master a few basic techniques during each session. Then it will be easier to focus on your training rather than trying to perform intricate combinations.

Although variety in your training is important, perfecting cardio kickboxing techniques means practice and repetition. It may take you one thousand repetitions to finally execute a perfect roundhouse kick. But don't be discouraged. This is one of the benefits of cardio kickboxing—you can always improve some aspect of your performance.

For example, you may spend an entire workout refining your roundhouse kicks and side kicks. (The difference between a roundhouse kick and a side kick is that the roundhouse kick comes from "around" whereas your side kick goes straight to your target. I talk more about kicks in Chapter 6). It takes some cardio kickboxers years to realize the difference between these two techniques.

If you are following an instructor, copy his or her moves. A mirror is also helpful. Don't watch your feet. If you watch your feet, or are not accustomed to training with a mirror, you may confuse which arm or leg is attacking and defending. And don't try to analyze too much. Simply follow. If you are a beginner, don't try to imitate complex techniques or combinations until you are comfortable with the basic techniques.

A great way to master the basics is through unilateral and bilateral training. Unilateral means focusing only on one side of your body, or just one limb. Bilateral means working both sides of your body or two limbs; for example, your left arm and right arm. Throw ten perfect left jabs (unilateral). Then execute ten perfect right jabs (unilateral). Then alternate with twenty left and right jabs consecutively (bilateral). Use this unilateral and bilateral strategy to learn all of your punches, kicks, strikes, and blocks.

More advanced techniques such as crescent kicks and swing kicks should be practiced slowly at first, and under the watchful eye of a qualified cardio kickboxing instructor.

Polish your cardio kickboxing form in front of a mirror or on a bag. Practicing your punching and kicking techniques on instructors or classmates is not allowed.

Cardio Kickbox at Your Own Pace

Throughout the book I will make reference to Level 1, 2, and 3 cardio kickboxers. This is an informal scale to help you decide what intensity to train at and what level of complexity to strive for. At all times, use your own best judgment in deciding how hard to train, and don't push yourself to injury. Use common sense and caution when trying any new technique.

- **Level 1 Cardio kickboxers—Sedentary.** Have not worked out in the past couple of years.
- **Level 2 Cardio kickboxers—Moderately Active.** Work out two or three times a week. Lead an active lifestyle.
- **Level 3 Cardio kickboxers—Very Active.** Work out three or four times a week at a vigorous level. Lead an active lifestyle.

Sticking with It

If you are just starting a cardio kickboxing program, the following tips may help you stick with the program.

Month 1: Make your cardio kickboxing program a habit.

1. Do not miss any scheduled workouts for your first month.
2. Clear your calendar to be sure of no conflicts.
3. If you dread cardio kickboxing, tell yourself you can quit after a month.
4. Reward yourself after each workout with a massage or hot bath.
5. After a month of cardio kickboxing, compare your fitness level from day one.

Month 2: Enjoy your training.

1. Introduce yourself to other cardio kickboxing enthusiasts.
2. Set realistic fitness goals based on your potential.
3. Ask a cardio kickboxing instructor about how you are progressing.

Month 3: Put your soul into your training.

1. Each time you cardio kickbox, work on a specific technique (for example, front kick, front punch).
2. Put your heart into your training.
3. Work on perfecting your weaker techniques.
4. Give one hundred percent of yourself to each of your workouts.
5. Practice the finer points (that is, hand positions and foot positions) of your cardio kickboxing techniques.

Chapter 2

Mind and Body

Cardio kickboxing® includes more than just punching and kicking. It is important to be relaxed and focused throughout your entire cardio kickboxing workout. This chapter will explain how to personalize your program to your personality and mindset. You will learn to breathe correctly and focus on the proper cues for exemplary performance.

Fuel the power of your techniques by talking to yourself effectively, visualizing your imaginary opponent, and associating with your muscles. And when your endorphins kick in, the fun is about to begin.

You can be a raging bull like Mike Tyson, throwing your punches with malicious intent. Or you may prefer the calm, effortless approach of an enlightened master like Kwai Chang Kane from the popular television show *Kung Fu.* Choose your mindset wisely.

Cardio kickboxing drills allow you to experience a series of extremes in a controlled setting. Repetitive unilateral kicks followed by slow shadowboxing brings you from one end of the intensity continuum to the other in seconds. Cardio kickboxing teaches you the flexibility to bend instead of break. If you plan to perform thirty consecutive unilateral side kicks, but the burn in your quadriceps becomes intense, you may enjoy the option of continuing with bilateral training.

The supple willow does not contend against the storm, yet it survives
—Lao Tzu

A cardio kickboxing workout is an excellent way to practice mindfulness. Mindfulness is simply concentrating on exactly what you are doing at the very moment you are doing it. Can you punch, and think of nothing but your punch? Most of us cannot, because we are not focused.

Meditation or walking for twenty minutes reduces stress, but cardio kickboxing goes a step further. Cardio kickboxing requires you to relax and focus on your imaginary opponent. This is mindfulness. Mindfulness allows you to relax. When you claim you don't have time to relax, that is when you need relaxation the most. Start by learning the relaxation techniques in the following section. Use them while cardio kickboxing until they become habit. Take these deep-breathing and tension-releasing exercises into your stress-filled life and use them anywhere, not just at the gym.

Relaxing During Cardio Kickboxing

You may ask, "Why should I relax while I'm working out?" That's a good question. When I say you should relax during your workout, I don't mean you should sit on your couch and put your feet up. I mean you should be alert and focused without unnecessary tension. With relaxation comes speed, increased efficiency, and power. Relaxation also allows for better agility and reaction time.

Try this relaxation exercise. Stand up with your feet a little more than shoulder width apart, toes pointing straight ahead. Bend your knees slightly, hold your abdominal muscles in, and let your shoulders drop. Keep your lower back flat, and tuck in your hips, as if you were about to sit in a chair (Figure 2-1). This is called "horse stance," one of the basic stances you'll learn in this book (see Chapter 4).

Figure 2-1

Now, relax your entire body except for the muscles that are holding you in place. Become especially aware of upper body tension and let those muscles relax. Release any tension in any part of your body. Don't force yourself to relax, just clear your mind and let it happen. When you relax, you will automatically punch and kick more easily and efficiently. And soon you will punch faster and harder because you are relaxed.

Focus on your breath. Hold your horse stance and breathe from your diaphragm instead of your chest. To do this, inhale from your nose to expand your lungs. Focus on raising your diaphragm. Fill your lower, central, and upper chest, in that order. Then take twice as long to exhale through your mouth and lower your diaphragm. Relax and breath for one to five minutes, letting all tension wash out of your body.

Mindfulness and Breathing

To combine mindfulness and breathing, get into your horse stance and take deep breaths from your diaphragm with long exhalations. After a minute, begin a punching drill. Exhale with each punch. Focus on your exhalation and let your punch occur automatically.

Now punch in double time, but stay mindful of your breath. Your breathing and heart rate increase. Your diaphragm expands with each inhalation. Imagine oxygen-filled blood cells nourishing your punching muscles. Exhale automatically. Release your punches with your full attention on what you are doing.

Similar to punching, mindfulness is a skill. The more you practice, the better your focus. But don't worry if you are a slow learner. Concern about your progress will impede your mindfulness.

Here's another exercise. Immerse yourself in music. Punch, kick, and relax simultaneously. Your music is your mantra. Each beat of the music serves to bring you further into relaxation. Mindfulness is not hard, but simply a matter of focusing on each punch and kick. Let distractions go in one ear and out the other. Continue punching and kicking and breathing at your own pace. Personalize it. The timing is yours, not an instructor's or a video's. Once you decide the level at which to perform, let nothing distract or disturb you; just punch, kick, and breathe. If thoughts or sounds interfere, notice them but let them go.

Association and Dissociation

Association and dissociation are mental techniques from sports psychology that can help you cardio kickbox more effectively. Association is similar to mindfulness. It simply means concentrating on feeling your muscles work. For instance, when you throw a punch, feel the energy in your muscles starting at your feet and traveling up through your leg and hip to your torso, and then out through your chest, shoulder, and arm in a perfect power chain.

Dissociation is the opposite of association. Rather than concentrate on your punch, distract yourself. Let music, a punching bag, or daydreaming pull you away from the present moment. Dissociation is a way to take your mind away from discomfort. It's a trick to keep you moving when you'd rather quit.

Use dissociation sparingly. You want to enjoy your workouts rather than distract yourself from them, and for safety reasons it's best to pay attention when cardio kickboxing. Also, don't use dissociation to distract yourself from a serious injury.

One-Minute Imagery Technique

Imagery is a great way to inspire yourself to work out. You can do it any time you need a mental boost to your spirits, or to prepare yourself for a cardio kickboxing session. Picture yourself cardio kickboxing. Several studies suggest that when you visualize yourself training, nervous impulses are sent down the proper neuromuscular pathways to stimulate your muscle fibers to enhance the speed and power of your kicks and punches. Stay relaxed when you practice this exercise. Imagery is most beneficial when performed consistently.

1. Close your eyes and relax (five seconds).
2. Breathe from your diaphragm. Focus on your breath (ten seconds).
3. See, feel, and experience yourself punching and kicking (thirty seconds).
4. Enjoy a sensation of perfect balance, control and heightened speed (ten seconds).
5. Slowly open your eyes (five seconds).

Setting Goals

Motivation for cardio kickboxing comes easily, for some. Your first step is to decide what you hope to accomplish—lose body fat, tone your muscles, or improve your cardiovascular system. Punch and kick until you meet some of your short-term goals. When you reach your long-term goals, you will feel successful.

Cardio kickboxing provides you with the opportunity to achieve fitness beyond your expectations. And you can enjoy the process. But first you must prepare. Close your eyes and take a few moments to determine your desires. How would it feel to gain strength and endurance and lose weight? Visualize yourself enjoying cardio kickboxing. Feel energy surging through your body.

After you decide your long-term goals, such as gaining strength and endurance, or losing weight, you need to set achievable short-term goals that will equip you to tackle your mission. If your short-term goal is to lose body fat, begin training slowly and then progress gradually. Perform bilateral punching and kicking for the first month. You can sprinkle some unilateral ten-repetition jabs into your program once a week if you feel frisky. After a month of training, if you feel ready, try unilateral ten-repetition kicks.

Daily short-term targets such as unilateral ten-repetition side kicks inspire you, and these early achievements serve as incentive. These small successes will provide endurance for the long haul. Begin with baby steps. After three months you may be ready for bilateral twenty-repetition kicks. And in six months you may attempt an astounding, bilateral, thirty-repetition kick program. Increase your intensity no more than five percent for a given workout. If you are too vigorous, your body and mind will revolt.

When you are performing a difficult drill, prepare for distractions and obstacles. Motivation waxes and wanes, and there will be pitfalls. Your body will find reasons to quit: you don't feel like sweating any more, you've had a long day at work, or you don't want to miss a favorite TV show. The secret is to convince yourself that cardio kickboxing is play. Also, keep your long-term goals (and the long-term benefits) in mind.

For instance, cardio kickboxing increases your strength, endurance, and flexibility. It also decreases your chances for heart disease, diabetes, and hypertension. Your energy and metabolism will increase, and your body fat, mid-afternoon lethargy, and mood swings will decrease. If you always look forward to cardio kickboxing you will never burn out. Cardio kickboxing is unique in that you can personalize your workout according to whether you are Level 1, Level 2, or Level 3. You decide when to challenge your body and when to relax.

The following checklist can help you meet your cardio kickboxing and fitness goals.
- Cardio kickbox daily with a clear, uncluttered mind. When you start your music, leave all distractions behind.
- Spend a few moments cardio kickboxing in goal-directed relaxation.
- Visualize your ideal self.
- Zero in on the goals you've set for yourself, such as becoming faster, healthier, or stronger.
- Adjust your goals to your capabilities.
- Visualize your goals and the training required to reach them.
- Evaluate your progress. If you reach a goal, set a new one.

Sticking to Your Program

There are no bad cardio kickboxing workouts. Some are more or less intense than others. A single session does not make or break your fitness. It is the dozens and hundreds of cardio kickboxing workouts that matter.

Enjoy deep levels of relaxation and concentration while punching and kicking. Cardio kickboxing opens capillaries and stimulates morphine-like pain killers called endorphins. Cardio kickboxing fanatics enjoy an "endorphin high."

If you have a cardio kickboxing workout scheduled but you feel sluggish, throw a few punches. Remember how good you feel about yourself at the end of a workout. Generally, following the warm-up, your endorphins kick in and you gladly complete your session.

Quitting is usually the first option when confronted with fatigue and discomfort. But to succeed, you must teach your body to handle discomfort a little at a time. Reach deep inside and ask a little more of yourself for each cardio kickboxing workout.

Expect to get through discomfort, but not pain. If you feel joint pain, change your technique to take the pressure off the painful joint. If you become lightheaded, slow down.

Psychological Strategies

Cardio kickboxing requires a narrow-internal focus of attention. Associate with your body by feeling every aspect of your punches and kicks.

Visualize muscle fibers splitting and blood pumping to your quadriceps, hamstrings, gluteals, gastrocnemius, and soleus. While associating with your muscles, you will find random thoughts will enter your mind in the form of self-talk.

Talk to yourself nicely. Self-talk takes the form of positive affirmations such as "Punching fast is easy." These self-verbalizations raise arousal levels. Although your arousal level may increase, relax your muscles. With relaxation comes speed and efficiency. Relax and notice if any of your muscles are tense and wasting precious energy.

Mental Toughness Tips

• Remain energized even when you are tired or discouraged.

• Act as if you are punching and kicking well even when you are not.

• Plan your strategy prior to each drill.

• Follow the same rituals before each cardio kickboxing workout.

• The faster and more furious you punch and kick with perfect form, the more you will love it.

• Have fun.

• Stay positive.

• By increasing awareness of your mental strengths and weaknesses, you'll be better equipped to consistently perform toward the upper range of your cardio kickboxing ability.

CHAPTER 3

Posture and Dynamic Stretching

To practice cardio kickboxing® safely, you must keep your back in proper alignment. Maintain a slight arch in your lower back (Figure 3-1). This slight arch is also known as a neutral spine. There is some debate as to whether you should bend your back or keep your posture erect when you kick. To me, there is no debate—keep your back as straight as you can.

In aerobics classes, instructors may have told you to "pull your belly button to your spine" to protect your lower back. Ironically it is not your abdominals that hold your belly button in, it is your diaphragm. A preferred guideline for cardio kickboxing is to maintain a neutral spine.

Sometimes you may experience lower back pain when training. Lower back pain may be caused by weakness in your abdominals or lower back muscles. It may be tightness in your hamstrings or hip flexors. Or you might have a structural problem such as scoliosis (S-curve), no curve, or bone degeneration.

Figure 3-1

Screenings such as trunk flexibility tests, hamstring flexibility tests, and bent knee curl up tests can help to determine the problem. A leg length discrepancy may cause pain on one side of your back. If ever you experience back pain while cardio kickboxing, see your physician.

In addition to maintaining a neutral spine, be sure and keep your upper body in proper fighting position when throwing all punches and kicks. That means keep your hands up near your face, with your elbows close to your body. Some enthusiasts have a tendency to let their arms flail wildly while focusing intensely on their kicks. Also, your knees and elbows should always be slightly bent (soft) during your workout.

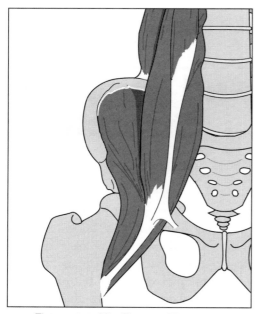

Figure 3-2. Hip Flexors (iliopsoas)

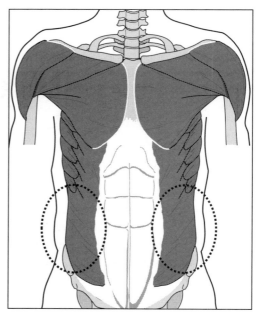

Figure 3-3. External and Internal Obliques

Core Muscles: Abs and Back

Be sure that your abdominals and back muscles are strong enough to support your cardio kickboxing routine. Test the balance of strength between your lower back and abdominal muscles by performing the following exercise. Lie on your back and keep your lower back flat while you extend your legs toward the ceiling. Slowly drop your legs while attempting to hold your lower back flat to the floor. If you can do this, your abdominals are strong enough to counter the pull from your hip flexors (Figure 3-2). Your hip flexors are extremely important for your cardio kickboxing. Each time you lift your knee, you innervate (that is, stimulate) your hip flexors.

Cardio kickboxing is great for your abdominal training. The workouts develop your entire torso. Every punch or kick you throw innervates your external and internal obliques, which are the abdominal muscles on the sides of your torso (Figure 3-3). When you throw a punch or a kick, an innertube-like contraction stabilizes your torso. When you contract your obliques you provide structural support to your spine, as if filling an innertube.

When you develop powerful obliques, you receive an added bonus of muscular love handles over your hips. Training obliques does not make your waist smaller. In fact if you overload your muscles, your waist may grow larger.

Figure 3-4

Figure 3-5

Dynamic Stretching

Advertisements in martial arts magazines suggest that in a few easy lessons, "you too can kick to head level, COLD!" Rather than risk a muscle strain or pull, I suggest that you warm up prior to performing ANY kick. And I also recommend that you try some of the dynamic stretches presented here.

These are not the traditional, static, reaching and pulling movements that you may have performed in the past while sitting on the floor. Static stretches are fine after your workout is completed, but research has demonstrated that static floor stretching does not necessarily translate into improved kicking flexibility.

Dynamic stretching utilizes your opposing muscle group (antagonist) to functionally stretch its agonist. For example, some of the dynamic stretches integrated into the cardio kickboxing program include slow, controlled, side leg raises and wall stretching exercises. These dynamic movements have been shown to improve kicking flexibility.

If you are interested in other flexibility exercises, I discuss additional stretching programs in my book *The Martial Arts Athlete*.

Stretch

Total time: five to eight minutes
1. Stand with your feet shoulder-width apart, knees slightly bent and hands at your sides. Take a deep breath and bring your arms up over your head. Exhale, and lower your arms back to your sides (Figure 3-4).
2. Place your hands on your hips and turn your head slowly from side to side, bringing your chin parallel with each of your shoulders (Figure 3-5).

Figure 3-6

Figure 3-7

3. Next, tilt your head from side to side so that your left ear almost touches your left shoulder and your right ear almost touches your right shoulder (Figure 3-6).

4. Shrug your shoulders up toward your ears. Then let your shoulders drop back to where they were. Repeat three times (Figure 3-7).

5. Windmill your shoulders and arms in a circular motion by bringing them forward, up, back, and down. Windmill ten times forward, then reverse directions and repeat ten times (Figure 3-8).

6. Stretch both of your arms in front of you, palms facing your chest. Interlock your fingers and round your upper back. You should feel a stretch in your upper back (Figure 3-9).

7. Interlock your fingers behind your back. Lift your hands back and up. You should feel a stretch in your upper chest and the front of your shoulders. Lift your arms as high as you comfortably can without leaning forward (Figure 3-10).

8. Extend your right heel out in front of you. Place your hands on your left leg, just above your knee. Slowly stretch the hamstring of your right leg by drawing your hips back. Switch legs and repeat (Figure 3-11).

Figure 3-8

Figure 3-9

Figure 3-10

Figure 3-11

Figure 3-12

Figure 3-13

9. Balance on your left leg and lift your right foot toward your buttocks. Gently grab the top of your right foot and pull your right heel toward your buttocks. Point your right knee down. Feel a stretch in your right quadriceps. Switch legs and repeat (Figure 3-12).

10. Step out to the side with your right leg and bend your knee. Shift your weight to your right leg and extend your left leg to the side. Feel a stretch in your right adductor muscles on the inside of your left thigh. Switch sides and repeat (Figure 3-13).

11. Step forward with your right foot and bend your knee. (Do not bend so far that you can no longer see your toes.) Gently twist your waist forward. Feel a stretch in your right hip flexor. Switch sides and repeat (Figure 3-14).

Figure 3-14

Tips on Stretching and Your Posture

1. Contract your abdominal muscles.
2. Maintain a neutral spine.
3. Lead with your chest, not with your head, when you stretch.
4. If you lose your form on your stretch, don't try to push any further.
5. Stretch after warming up.
6. Never hold your breath on your stretches.
7. Breathe from your diaphragm throughout your entire stretching routine.
8. Relax and breathe into your muscles on each stretch.

CHAPTER 4

Stance Training

All the power in your techniques is generated from your legs and hips. Stance training will give you a strong base of support from which to throw powerful punches, kicks, and blocks. The following stances are also the foundation for moving and stepping in cardio kickboxing, which I discuss in Chapter 8.

Some of these postures may feel awkward at first. With a little practice, they'll become natural and comfortable. Maintain perfect posture on all of your stances. Keep your eyes up, your back neutral, your shoulders even, your stomach in, and your knees bent.

Level 1 cardio kickboxers should not hold each stance for more than ten seconds. As your strength improves, you can try holding each stance between thirty seconds and one minute.

Horse Stance

Stand with your feet shoulder-width apart, toes pointed straight ahead, knees slightly bent, as if you were riding a horse (Figure 4-1). Bend your knees so a string dropped from each of your knees would hit your big toes. Keep your hips tucked as if you were about to sit down, and contract your abdominals. Keep your back straight. Pulse two inches up and down to the beat of your music while keeping your feet flat on the floor. This exercise trains your quadriceps, glutes, and hamstrings.

Square Stance

Change your feet from the horse stance to a square stance. Open your legs a bit wider than horse stance, and point your toes out at about a forty-five degree angle. Bend both knees and keep your back straight (Figure 4-2). Pulse up and down to the beat while keeping your feet flat on the floor. This exercise works your quadriceps, glutes, and hamstrings.

Square Stance Heels Off

This is the same as the square stance, except now you lift your heels off of the floor (Figure 4-3). This exercise is good muscular endurance training for your upper and lower legs. It is great for the quadriceps, glutes, hamstrings, and the lower leg muscles.

Front Stance

Step forward with your right leg into a front stance. Your right knee and foot should point straight ahead. Do not let your right knee go beyond your toes. Keep your back leg

Figure 4-1

Figure 4-2

Figure 4-3

Figure 4-4

straight but do not lock your left knee (Figure 4-4). Transfer your weight to your right leg and pulse two inches up and down. Switch sides and continue pulsing. This exercise works your quadriceps, adductors, and hamstrings.

Figure 4-5

Figure 4-6

Front Stance Balance

Step into a front stance with your right leg. Bend your right knee and lift your left leg off the floor. Balance on one leg and pulse gently, keeping your weight over your right knee (Figure 4-5). Keep your back leg straight. If necessary, use a wall for balance. You don't have to lift your back leg very high. Switch legs and repeat. The front stance balance works the glutes of your back leg, the quadriceps of your front leg, and auxiliary muscles used to maintain your balance.

Cat Stance

Switch from your front stance to a cat stance by shifting seventy percent of your weight to your back foot. Balance the remainder of your weight on the ball of your front foot (Figure 4-6). Focus your attention on gently pulsing your back leg. Switch legs and repeat. The cat stance works the upper part of your back leg, and the soleus muscle of your front leg.

Front Stance Knee Down

Go back into a front stance with your left leg forward. Bend your right knee so that it comes within one inch of the floor (Figure 4-7). Pulse two inches up and down. This exercise trains your quadriceps, glutes, hamstrings, and stabilizer muscles. Switch legs and repeat.

Figure 4-7

Figure 4-8

Hourglass Stance

Start with your feet shoulder-width apart. Turn your toes slightly inward. Keep your knees over your toes (Figure 4-8). Pulse up and down gently. This exercise works your outer thigh muscles.

Fighting Stance

From your hourglass stance, pivot on your heels so your toes are pointing at a forty-five degree angle to the front. Keep your hands up in front of your body (Figure 4-9). Pulse up and down. The fighting stance is excellent for training your inner thigh muscles. Get used to this posture—a good portion of your cardio kickboxing workout uses this stance.

Figure 4-9

CHAPTER 5

Punches and Strikes

When you punch, begin slowly. Move through a full range of motion on each technique. At first pay attention to form without concern for overall performance. After you have learned the movements, increase your speed and intensity.

Whenever you make a fist, be sure that you roll your fingers tightly together so your hands are protected. Press your thumbs tightly against your index and middle fingers on the outside of your fist. Keep your elbows slightly bent (soft) on all punches and strikes.

Front Punch

Begin in a horse stance. Make fists with both hands and hold them at your waist. Punch with your left hand out to the front (Figure 5-1). The palm of your left hand should face the floor. Retract your left hand to your waist and punch with your right hand at the same time, in a piston-like motion, striking with the first two knuckles. Use this complementary movement for each repetition. A common error is to push your punch. Learn to relax so that your arms feel like strings with fists attached. Keep your knees bent and your back straight in a solid horse stance.

Figure 5-1

Hook Punch

Begin in a fighting position. Keep your hands up (Figure 5-2). Deliver the hook punch with your front hand, and keep your back hand up and close to your chin. As you punch, your front elbow comes up and is parallel to the floor (Figure 5-3). Hit with your first two knuckles. Your palm faces the floor at contact. The hook is a solid, in-close assault. Keep it tight. Don't swing wide. The power in your hook is generated from your feet, through your hip, to your shoulder, and out your arm.

Figure 5-2

Figure 5-3

Jab

The jab is a fast, front-hand strike. It is not as powerful as the hook, but it is particularly useful for setting up another, more powerful blast such as a front kick or reverse punch. Begin in a fighting stance with your front arm bent (Figure 5-4). Keep your elbow in close to guard your body. Quickly shoot your fist forward to your target; that is, an imaginary opponent's nose. Twist your wrist so your palm is facing down at contact (Figure 5-5). Hit with your first two knuckles. Bring your hand back as quickly as it was extended (Figure 5-6).

Elbow

The elbow strike is a remarkably powerful technique. Begin in a fighting position (Figure 5-7). Strike with either elbow. Twist your hips and pivot on your front heel from a fighting

Figure 5-4

stance into a front stance and transfer your weight into the strike (Figure 5-8). Cup your free hand over your fist for additional power. The elbow strike can be employed from a variety of angles: across into the face; back to the temple; straight up into the solar plexus; down to the face, throat, or collarbone; or directly behind you into the solar plexus.

Figure 5-5

Figure 5-6

Figure 5-7

Figure 5-8

Figure 5-9

Figure 5-10

Chop

Begin in a horse stance with your hands up in a fighting position. Lift your open hand to your ear as if preparing to throw a ball. Shoot it straight toward the neck of your imaginary opponent, twisting your hand just before contact so that your palm is facing upward (Figure 5-9). Strike with the meaty portion of the side of your hand between the wrist and the joint of your little finger. Simultaneously retract your other hand back. Strike horizontally to the neck of your imaginary opponent. Snap your wrist at the end of your attack for added speed and power.

Palm Heel

Begin in a horse stance with your elbows in and your hands up in a fighting position. Aim the lower part of your palm (called the palm heel or base of the palm) to the solar plexus or nose of your imaginary opponent (Figure 5-10). At the same time, pull your other hand back to your torso. You can add power to the technique by twisting your hips as you strike. Begin a power surge from your feet that travels through your body and is channeled into the palm.

Reverse Punch

The rear hand reverse punch is your most powerful strike. It is a very graceful, flowing technique using your entire body. Start from a fighting stance (Figure 5-11) and pivot into a front stance. Simultaneously twist your hip, letting loose a power chain that explodes out as your back hand shoots forward (Figure 5-12). Your weight shifts from your rear foot to your front foot prior to contact. Remain relaxed until the moment of impact. Use the first two

Figure 5-11

Figure 5-12

knuckles for penetration and a twist of the wrist for torque. Retract your opposite hand toward your chin to protect yourself from a counterattack.

Backfist Strike

The backfist strike is a fast, front-hand technique thrown from a fighting position. It is similar to a jab except that it moves horizontal to the target. Place your hands in a fighting position with your elbows bent and your arms relaxed (Figure 5-13). Move your fist in a slapping motion toward your target. Be careful not to telegraph by lifting your elbow. Make contact with your first two knuckles (Figure 5-14). Retract your hand quickly back to your fighting position. You can throw a backfist punch either in a parallel or downward motion.

Figure 5-13

Figure 5-14

Figure 5-15

Ridge Hand Strike

Begin in a horse stance. One hand shoots forward, using the inside portion of your hand between your thumb and index finger as the striking surface (Figure 5-15). Your other hand comes up to protect your body. The ridge hand strike is thrown exactly like a hook except you extend your elbow just before contact.

Spear Hand

Begin in a horse stance with your hands open, fingers held together. Throw your spear hand exactly like a punch, but strike with the ends of your fingers (Figure 5-16). Be sure to make the ends of the three striking fingers flush to your imaginary target, which can be the eyes, the throat, or the solar plexus.

Forearm Strike

Begin in a fighting stance. Swing your back arm in a wide arcing circle while protecting your body and face with your front hand (Figure 5-17). The forearm is primarily used for blocking, but it can also strike the neck and face of your opponent at close range. You may use the outer or inner forearm as the striking surface.

Back Punch Twist

Begin in a horse stance with your hands at your waist. Look over your left shoulder and execute a punch behind you with your right arm (Figure 5-18). Then look over your right shoulder and punch with your left arm. Retract each non-punching arm to your torso.

Figure 5-16

Figure 5-17

Figure 5-18

Figure 5-19

Side Twist Punch

Begin in a horse stance with your fists at your sides. Look to your left as you twist your waist and throw a right punch to the side (Figure 5-19). Retract your left arm to your torso. Then look to your right and punch with your left arm. Retract your right arm into a fighting position.

CHAPTER 6

Kicks

Always begin your kicking program easily and slowly. Move through a full range of motion on each technique. Watch your form without concern about overall performance. Don't worry about height and speed until you master the basic movements. After you have learned to kick properly, then you can increase your speed, intensity, and height.

Be sure to warm up before doing any kicking drills. Keep your knees bent on all of your kicks and never fully extend your knee joint.

Front Kick

The front kick has five steps. Begin in a standing position with your weight equally distributed. Raise your right foot to knee height and point your kicking knee at your target (Figure 6-1). Chamber the heel of your kicking foot as close to your hip as possible (Figure 6-2). Extend your foot straight to your imaginary target (Figure 6-3). Pull your toes back and strike with the ball of the foot (Figure 6-4). Bring your foot back to your knee (Figure 6-5). Set your foot down on the floor in a controlled fashion. Switch sides and repeat.

Figure 6-1

Figure 6-2

Figure 6-3

Figure 6-4

Figure 6-5

Figure 6-6

Roundhouse Kick

The roundhouse kick has four steps. Begin in a standing position with your weight equally distributed. Raise your right leg so that the side of your knee is almost parallel to the floor (Figure 6-6). Your heel is chambered close to your hip, which is also known as the fold

Figure 6-7

Figure 6-8

position. Snap your foot forward from the fold position horizontally to your target (Figure 6-7). Your leg should come around in a half-circle. Twist your hips for added power. Strike with the ball of your foot, the top of your foot or with your toe if you are wearing cross-training shoes. Retract your foot back to your knee, then lower your foot gently to the floor. Switch sides and repeat.

Side Kick

Begin in a standing position with your weight equally distributed. Raise your foot to knee level (Figure 6-8). Chamber your foot in a position so it is protecting your groin. Keep your back upright until the last second and then extend your foot sideways to the target (Figure 6-9). Twist your hip for added power. Hit fast and hard, slicing through the imaginary target with your heel. Retract your foot to your knee and set your foot down with control. Switch sides and repeat.

Figure 6-9

The difference between the side kick and the roundhouse kick is that the side kick shoots in a straight line forward, while the roundhouse kick swings in a half circle around toward your target.

Figure 6-10

Figure 6-11

Side-Hook Kick

Begin in a standing position with your weight evenly distributed. Lift your knee to your chest as if to execute a side kick (Figure 6-10). Instead of shooting straight forward, hook your kick sideways to the imaginary target (Figures 6-11 and 6-12). Strike with the back of your heel. Bring your foot back to the chambered position as quickly as you can (Figure 6-13). Set your foot down on the floor. Switch sides and repeat.

Knee Strike

As with elbow strikes, knee strikes are used when you are in close range with your imaginary opponent. The groin is the primary target, but the solar plexus and even the face are possible targets if you can grab your imaginary opponent and pull him or her into the strike.

Figure 6-12

Begin in a front stance with your arms open (Figure 6-14). Lift your knee up hard and fast toward your imaginary target while pulling down with your hands (Figure 6-15). Do not bend at the waist. Shoot your knee into the striking area and then step down as quickly as possible. Switch sides and repeat.

Figure 6-13

Figure 6-14

Figure 6-15

Figure 6-16

Jump Kicks

Jump kicks should only be performed by Level 3 cardio kickboxers. Start with your left leg forward in a fighting stance (Figure 6-16). Jump up with your right leg. Raise it quickly so that your left foot leaves the floor (Figure 6-17). While in the air, use your left leg to throw

Figure 6-17

Figure 6-18

a front kick, side kick or roundhouse kick (Figure 6-18). Land gracefully on both feet with your knees soft. Switch sides and repeat.

CHAPTER 7

Blocks

Blocks are your basic method of self-defense, and an important part of your cardio kick-boxing® workout. In later chapters you'll learn to combine blocks with punches and kicks.

Keep your elbows slightly bent (soft) on all of your blocks.

Knife-Hand Block

Begin in a left front stance with your hands up. Bring both arms toward your left shoulder with your palms facing your head (Figure 7-1). Stay sideways as you whip both arms forward to block (Figure 7-2). Knock the imaginary body punch away with your right hand and guard your solar plexus with your left. Keep your elbows bent at ninety degrees. Stay relaxed throughout the movement and contract your muscles at the completion of the block. Switch sides and repeat.

Figure 7-1

Figure 7-2

Figure 7-3

Figure 7-4

Overhead Block

Begin in a left front stance with your hands crossed in front of your sternum, left hand over right (Figure 7-3). Raise your right arm up past your face to block an imaginary punch. Twist your arm so that as it reaches your forehead and your palm faces your imaginary opponent. At the same time, retract your left fist to your torso (Figure 7-4). Remain relaxed until the completion of the block. Switch sides and repeat.

Inner Block

Begin in a horse stance with your hands in a fighting position. Raise your right fist up to your ear with your palm facing your opponent. Your elbow should be parallel to your shoulder (Figure 7-5). Twist your hips and pivot on your feet into a forty-five degree left

Figure 7-5

front stance. Bring your arm sharply across your body, twisting your palm so it faces your midsection at the conclusion of the block. Retract your left fist to your torso as you block

Figure 7-6

Figure 7-7

(Figure 7-6). Imagine the punch coming at your midsection. Contract your muscles at contact. Switch sides and repeat.

Downward Block

Begin in a left front stance with your hands in a fighting position. Raise your right fist over your left shoulder with your palm facing your ear (Figure 7-7). Sweep your arm downward across your body, striking with the outside of your forearm. Retract your left fist to your torso at the same time. Finish with your right fist six inches above your knee (Figure 7-8). Your elbow should be slightly bent at the completion of the block. Imagine you are blocking a kick to your lower body. Relax all of your muscles until contact. Switch sides and repeat.

Figure 7-8

Figure 7-9

Figure 7-10

Blocking a Kick

Begin in a horse stance with your hands in a fighting position. As your imaginary opponent attempts a roundhouse kick to your groin, pivot on your left foot as you lift up your right knee. You will take the imaginary kick on your right shin as your right arm reinforces the block and your left arm protects your solar plexus (Figure 7-9). Your right leg is now in position to counterattack with a side kick. Switch sides and repeat.

Slipping a Punch

The best block is to get out of the way! Move your head to the left or to the right to evade an imaginary punch to the face (Figure 7-10). Wait until you imagine the direction of the attack before you begin your movement. Always use one hand to protect your face and the other to protect your midsection.

Duck Under

Imagine someone throwing a hook punch at your head. Duck under the punch by bending at the knees while keeping your eyes focused on the solar plexus of your imaginary opponent (Figure 7-11). Keep your hands up in a fighting position to reinforce your block, and don't bend your back.

Lean

Lean away from an imaginary attack just far enough to be out of reach (Figure 7-12).

Figure 7-11

Figure 7-12

Figure 7-13

Figure 7-14

Downward Block of a Center Punch

Begin in a left front stance with your hands in a fighting position. Raise your right arm with your fist at eye level (Figure 7-13). Twist your hips as you swing your arm down toward your midsection, blocking an imaginary strike to your belly (Figure 7-14). Swing your arm

Figure 7-15

Figure 7-16

down so that your elbow is at a ninety degree angle at about belt level. Switch sides and repeat.

Punching a Kick

Begin in a horse stance with your hands in a fighting position. Thrust your left hand down as if punching a kick to your groin. At the same time, retract your right hand to your torso (Figure 7-15). You can also use this block in a front stance (Figure 7-16). Remain relaxed through the duration of the technique until the moment you make contact. At that moment, focus your power into the block. Switch sides and repeat.

Blocking a Punch-Kick Combination

Begin in a left front stance with your hands up. Raise your right arm parallel to your face with your hand open, and block an imaginary head punch (Figure 7-17). Sweep your hand downward to block your imaginary opponent's kick to the body (Figure 7-18). While you swing your arm down, twist your hips into the block to protect your groin and add power to the block. Switch sides and repeat.

Catching a Kick

Begin in a horse stance with your hands by your waist (Figure 7-19). Imagine your opponent throws a front kick at your belly. Twist your hips and pivot on your feet into a left front stance and scoop with your right arm until it forms a ninety degree angle at the elbow, with your palm facing the ceiling. Simultaneously retract your left arm to your torso (Figure 7-20). Imagine catching your opponent's leg as you twist. Switch sides and repeat.

Figure 7-17

Figure 7-18

Figure 7-19

Figure 7-20

Figure 7-21

Figure 7-22

Bob and Weave

Begin in a fighting position. Imagine your opponent punches at your head. Move to your left to avoid the punch (Figure 7-21). Then quickly bend your knees to avoid a hook (Figure 7-22). Keep your hands up in a fighting position. When you come up again, shift to the right (Figure 7-23). Repeat.

X-Block

Begin in a horse stance. Block a high strike from your imaginary opponent by raising your arms above your head and crossing your wrists so that your forearms catch the blow (Figure 7-24). Immediately block a strike to your groin by dropping your hands and crossing them, so that your forearms stop the imaginary kick (Figure 7-25).

Figure 7-23

Figure 7-24

Figure 7-25

CHAPTER 8

Footwork

Footwork is essential in cardio kickboxing®. Along with stances, footwork is a foundation on which to build your techniques. Footwork, also known as shuffling or stepping, develops your agility, speed, and coordination. It also keeps you moving as you work out.

Keep your shoulders level and your knees soft as you step and shuffle. Never cross your legs. The reason is that your imaginary opponent could knock you off balance if you crossed your legs during an attack or defensive move. The only time you are permitted to cross your feet is during a cross-behind side kick, or cross-in-front roundhouse kick. You can cross your feet on these attacks because your momentum will carry you in the direction of your kick. Following your side kick or roundhouse kick, it is important to once again establish a solid base of support.

Shuffle

Begin in a fighting position with your left foot forward (Figure 8-1). Quickly slide your right foot forward until it touches the inside of your left foot (Figure 8-2). Plant your right

Figure 8-1

Figure 8-2

Figure 8-3

Figure 8-4

foot and quickly slide your left foot back so that you are now in a fighting stance with your right foot forward. Switch sides and repeat. When moving forward or backward, your head, chest and hips should remain level. Practice this until you can shuffle and change your feet very quickly.

Step

Begin in a left foot forward fighting position (Figure 8-3). Step forward with your right foot so that you are in a right foot forward fighting position (Figure 8-4). Repeat. This technique can be combined with the shuffle.

Front Stance, Step

Begin in a left front stance (Figure 8-5). Bring your right foot up and touch with the ball of your right foot next to your left (front) foot (Figure 8-6). Quickly shift into a right front stance (Figure 8-7).

Cat Stance, Step

Begin in a cat stance with your back leg supporting seventy percent of your weight. The toes of your back foot are pointed at a forty-five degree angle to the front. Your front foot is positioned so that your ankle is flexed and the ball of your foot rests on the floor and supports the remaining thirty percent of your weight (Figure 8-8). Push off with your back foot and step forward heel-to-toe with your front foot (Figure 8-9), then settle into your cat stance again (Figure 8-10).

Figure 8-5

Figure 8-6

Figure 8-7

Figure 8-8

Figure 8-9

Figure 8-10

Horse Stance, Pivot to Front Stance

Begin in a horse stance with your feet shoulder width apart and both knees bent. Your knees should be slightly bowed out as if riding a horse (Figure 8-11). Pivot on both feet into a front stance (Figure 8-12). Next, twist your hips and pivot your feet into a front stance in the other direction. Switch sides and repeat.

Touch Step

Begin in a horse stance (Figure 8-13). Raise your right foot so that it touches the inside of your left knee (Figure 8-14), then quickly return to horse stance. Repeat the same motion with your left foot. Continue moving side to side until the movements are quick and natural.

Figure 8-11

Cross Step

With your weight evenly distributed in a fighting stance (Figure 8-15), switch foot positions simultaneously (Figure 8-16), letting your feet skim quickly above the floor. The cross

Figure 8-12

Figure 8-13

Figure 8-14

Figure 8-15

step (also known as the Ali shuffle) can be used as a fake, or it may be followed by a rear leg kick. After you are comfortable with this single cross step, you can do multiple cross steps; that is, as soon as your feet touch the floor, switch back to your original position.

Figure 8-16

Figure 8-17

Slide Step Forward from a Fighting Stance

Begin in a fighting stance (Figure 8-17). Slide your back foot toward your front foot by gripping the floor with the ball of your front foot and pulling your rear foot forward (Figure 8-18). As your back foot comes up, step forward with your right foot into your fighting stance (Figure 8-19). Do this as quickly as you can. Keep your shoulders and hips level throughout. Your knees should be bent at all times.

Push-Slide

The push-slide is the most deceptive method of closing the distance between yourself and your opponent. Start in a fighting stance (Figure 8-20). Lift your front knee and let it pull you forward (Figure 8-21). Drop your foot and return to your fighting stance. If

Figure 8-18

you wish to move backward, lift your rear foot slightly off the floor and push off your front foot. Keep your shoulders level and your arms up so as not to telegraph your intentions.

Figure 8-19

Figure 8-20

Figure 8-21

Figure 8-22

Switch

Begin in a fighting position with your right foot forward (Figure 8-22). Jump up so that both feet barely leave the ground (Figure 8-23) and switch your feet as quickly as you can in the air. Land in a fighting position with your left foot forward (Figure 8-24). Switch sides and

Figure 8-23

Figure 8-24

repeat. This technique is similar to the cross step, except that in this case you jump off the ground. In the cross step, your feet skim just above the floor without leaving the ground.

Cross Walk

From your fighting stance, cross one leg behind the other one and bend both knees (Figure 8-25). Walk the length of the practice floor, keeping your knees bent throughout the exercise. The cross walk works your quadriceps and the muscles of your inner and outer thighs.

Figure 8-25

CHAPTER 9

Intensity

A great characteristic of cardio kickboxing® is that you can modify your intensity. Intensity is evaluated as a measure of your heart rate, how your muscles feel, and how you feel in general. Do not compare your intensity to someone else. If someone else can do repeated kicking drills at high intensity and you can only manage a knee lift, that is fine.

Choose to kick and punch to the chest, body, or knee of your imaginary opponent depending on how you feel. Compete only against yourself. Flexibility for high or low kicking varies depending on your age, fitness level, gender, and genetics. Also, if cardio kickboxing is a new skill for you, begin slowly and work on your form. Gradually, your fitness level and skill level will increase to levels you never thought possible.

There are six ways to modify intensity when cardio kickboxing.

1. **Change kicking height**. The first way to heighten or reduce intensity is to change the height of your kicks. For example, kicking to knee level is easier than kicking to the chest.

2. **Speed up or slow down.** The second way to alter your intensity is to speed up or slow down your punches and kicks. Adding more speed to your movements will increase the intensity of the drill. Always make sure you are in control if you are speeding up.

3. **Mix bilateral and unilateral drills.** To increase intensity, throw consecutive punches and kicks with the same arm or leg (unilateral). For example, throw ten jabs with your right hand. This is more difficult than alternating your techniques (for example, throwing a right jab and then a left jab). Bilateral drills give each limb a chance to rest between techniques.

4. **Use mindful focus and breathing drills.** The fourth way to modify intensity is through mindful focus and breathing drills. When you focus your mind on an exciting thought, such as squaring off with an imaginary opponent, you stimulate your body into an arousal state which will help to increase intensity slightly.

   To decrease intensity, you can use the following breathing drill, which is also used to help you recover after a tough workout. It works like this: Focus on a long exhalation through your mouth, and a shorter inhalation through your nose. This breathing drill helps to calm your body by delivering more oxygen to your working muscles.

5. **Alternate larger and smaller muscle groups.** Throwing a kick demands more energy than executing a jab. Chambering your leg requires more energy than throwing a punch.

6. **Increase or decrease your power.** Increasing the power in your kicks, punches and blocks will increase the intensity of your workout. Power is a function of speed and mass. Therefore, to create more power, you have to increase your speed. But remain relaxed between your cardio kickboxing techniques to increase the speed and power of your next effort. To reduce intensity, reduce the power in your techniques—but do not let your form get sloppy. Knowing how hard and how fast to punch and kick is important. Sometimes you punch and kick too vigorously and discover you are overtraining. But if you don't move fast enough, you may not achieve your fitness and performance goals.

Cardio Kickboxing and Cardiovascular Exercise

If your goal is to be fit and healthy, cardiovascular (CV) exercise is an important step. CV exercise combats obesity, high blood pressure, and glucose intolerance. Twenty minutes of cardio kickboxing, three or four times a week, is an effective way to improve the efficiency of your CV system.

Your CV system includes your heart, lungs, circulatory system, and tiny capillaries that supply oxygen and energy to your muscles. As your CV system improves, you burn fat more efficiently. Your body will be transformed into an aerobic furnace.

If you are punching and kicking in your target heart rate zone, your exercise is aerobic. Your blood delivers a continuous supply of oxygen to your punching and kicking muscles. Punching and kicking at a constant pace for twenty minutes is an example of aerobic exercise. There is evidence that cardio kickboxing at a consistent speed for as little as ten minutes can improve your cardiovascular endurance.

A great training effect of cardio kickboxing is that your resting heart rate will generally slow. In fact, cardio kickboxing may give you a stronger heart, providing for a greater stroke volume (which means you eject more blood through your body with each beat). You may notice an increase in energy, which will enable you to work longer and harder without fatigue.

Interval training will also improve your aerobic capacity, which is your body's ability to deliver oxygen to your punching and kicking muscles. VO_2 maximum (max.) is the greatest amount of oxygen your body can take in and use to provide energy to your muscles during your best effort. In other words, it is the rate your quadriceps, hamstrings, gluteals, and calf muscles efficiently use nutrients to power your kicks. The faster your body can deliver oxygen to your kicking muscles, the higher your VO_2 max.

You can improve your VO_2 max. by about twenty percent, but the remainder of it depends on your genetics. But part of improving your VO_2 max. depends on how you tolerate lactic acid.

Lactic acid is that searing sensation you feel in your legs when you perform thirty consecutive side kicks. Interval training increases your ability to tolerate lactic acid and therefore enhances your VO_2 max.

Heart Rate

When putting together your cardio kickboxing workouts, it is important that you understand your body's signals, and how those signals adapt and relate to the punches and kicks that you are performing.

Your heart rate is one way to measure intensity, and to notice changes in your fitness and health levels. Once you determine your resting heart rate and training heart rate, it will be easy to discover if you are cardio kickboxing too hard or not hard enough. After a few months of training, you will be amazed that you will probably be able to estimate your heart rate within a couple of beats.

For example, when you warm up, your heart rate may average around one hundred beats per minute. But when you accelerate into combinations, you will perceive that you are exerting more, and you are. Your training heart rate will correlate quite closely with how you feel.

Resting Heart Rate

Your resting heart rate (RHR) is your body's heart rate at rest, or your pulse rate taken approximately one hour before your normal waking time. Three ways to determine your resting heart rate are:

1. Have someone gently wake you, and then take your pulse one hour before your normal waking time. Count your pulse for one minute.
2. In the evening, lie down on your back and allow your body to relax without any distractions. Breathe comfortably for twenty to thirty minutes. Count your pulse for one minute.
3. Wear a heart rate monitor to sleep and glance at it just as you are starting to wake. Record this number seven days in a row. Add them together, and divide by seven. This will give you a true average of your RHR.

If you regularly record this figure and notice that your numbers are increasing by ten percent, it means you are overtraining, overstressed, or your body is starting to break down and you could be getting ill. If you notice this happening, take the day off to rest.

On the other hand, if you notice your RHR dropping slightly, this is one indication that your cardiovascular fitness level is improving. It means your heart has to beat fewer times each minute to sustain your normal body functions.

Maximum Heart Rate

Your maximum heart rate (MHR) is the maximum number of times your heart contracts in a given minute.

There are two ways to determine your MHR:

1. Use this age-predicted formula. Men should subtract their age from 220. The result is the MHR. Women should subtract their age from 226. This is an easy, somewhat accurate way to determine your MHR.

2. Undergo a maximum stress test performed by a physician in a clinical setting. This is a more precise measure of MHR. A maximum stress test requires you to walk on a treadmill while a doctor measures your vital signs. The walk turns into a jog, and then a run as the treadmill speeds up and the grade increases. The object is to push yourself to your physical limit. At the moment you reach your limit, the doctor records your maximum heart rate.

Recovery Heart Rate

Your recovery heart rate is your heart rate measured two minutes after you complete a workout. Determine your recovery heart rate by counting your pulse for one minute. The difference between recovery heart rate and resting heart rate is that your recovery measure is taken after exercise.

Record your recovery heart rate frequently—it's another method of determining cardio-vascular fitness. The quicker the number drops the better your fitness level. And the sooner it drops, the quicker you can perform another drill or interval of cardio kickboxing.

If you are a Level 1 (beginning) cardio kickboxer and have not exercised regularly, I rec-ommend that you stay in the lower heart rate zones for the first two weeks. Work out two or three times per week for a maximum of twenty minutes. This allows for an easy break-in peri-od that will help ward off excessive soreness. You may progress to higher levels as you feel comfortable, or as prescribed by your doctor or certified fitness professional.

If you are a Level 2 cardio kickboxer, which means you have been exercising regularly a minimum of two times a week and lead an active lifestyle, you can cardio kickbox two or three times a week for a maximum of thirty to forty minutes. Feel free to spend sixty to eighty per-cent of your workout in your higher heart rate zone. A good rule of thumb is if you perform two four-minute drills in a higher zone, then perform one drill in a lower zone to help recover.

If you are a Level 3 cardio kickboxer, which means you have been exercising regularly and vigorously three or more times a week, and you lead an active lifestyle, you can cardio kickbox three or more times a week for forty to sixty minutes. Feel free to spend seventy to eighty percent of your workout in your higher heart rate zone. If you perform two (or three) four-minute drills in a higher zone, then perform one drill in the lower zone to recover.

Cardio Kickboxing and Your Metabolism

You know that you burn calories during your cardio kickboxing workout. But depend-ing on the intensity of your workout, you can burn calories hours after you are done! This is because your heart rate and respiration remain elevated, increasing your basal metabolic rate. While you are punching and kicking, your body burns carbohydrates rather than fat. But while your feet are propped comfortably on the couch afterward, your fat stores release ener-gy to replace depleted carbohydrates.

EPOC, or excess post oxygen consumption, is the "afterburn," or the total number of calories you burn long after you complete your workout. Studies show that you can increase EPOC for up to sixteen hours after a workout. The number of total calories you burn is dependent on the amount of work performed, regardless of whether it was continuous or intermittent. Interval cardio kickboxing, which allows you to perform more "work," increases your EPOC.

Cardio Kickboxing and Interval Training

Years ago, fitness enthusiasts were instructed to gradually increase exercise intensity until they reached a steady state. Steady state refers to a target heart rate just below anaerobic threshold (that is, just before lactic acid accumulates in your muscles and you "feel the burn"). The goal was to endure this level of intensity for as long as possible.

Recently however, research has shown it is better to vary the intensity of a workout through interval training. Interval training means changing your intensity throughout your workout, alternating periods of high-intensity exercise with periods of low-intensity exercise.

Interval training cardio kickboxing drills burn fat and build endurance, speed, and recovery. And interval training makes for a pleasant change of pace. The faster, more intense, and challenging kicks may be exhilarating yet uncomfortable at first. Your heart rate and breathing will skyrocket; your thighs will feel rubbery. But after a couple of months, intervals are energizing.

But before moving to interval workouts, I want to discuss shadowboxing and cooling down.

Shadowboxing

Shadowboxing is a spontaneous display of punches, kicks, strikes, and blocks. Shadowboxing is a great way to transition between drills, or to give yourself a rest without completely stopping your workout. You can shadowbox at high and low intensities, depending on how you feel.

Slow Shadowboxing (Low Intensity)

Begin by facing a mirror in a fighting stance. Throw slow, low, bilateral front kicks. Then alternate slow and low roundhouse kicks. And finally, throw slow, low side kicks with each leg. Mix easy punches into your kicking combinations. Kick and punch with control. Keep your upper body relaxed and in perfect fighting position. Practice in superslow motion. This aids your balance.

> ## Shadowboxing Checklist
> - Keep your elbows in, chin down, and hands up.
> - Chamber your knee high enough on your side kick so that your foot travels travel straight to your target.
> - Be light on your feet.
> - Do not overextend on any of your punches or kicks.
> - Check your balance.
> - Focus your eyes on the solar plexus of your imaginary opponent.
> - Let your combinations flow.
> - Keep your elbows and knees soft (relaxed).

Fast Shadowboxing (High Intensity)

After you warm up, increase the trajectory of your kicks. Kick higher and faster. Alternate legs. Next throw unilateral repeaters. Try the same kick ten times in a row at fast speed. Mix all of your kicks at every height and angle. Add fast punches into the mix.

Figure 9-1

Figure 9-2

Special Cooldown

Cooling down, which you should do at the end of every workout, is essential to help your body transition from energy expenditure to recovery. The following cooldown is a restful, relaxing way to finish off a training session. You can also use it any time you need to relax, relieve stress or refresh yourself.

Level 1. Begin in a horse stance. Place your hands on an imaginary table top in front of you (Figure 9-1). Touch the roof of your mouth with the tip of your tongue. Inhale very slowly from your diaphragm. At the same time, raise your arms as if helium balloons were lifting your wrists (Figure 9-2). When your arms reach chest level, begin your exhalation. As you exhale, slowly lower your arms until your hands are resting on your imaginary table top. Repeat ten times.

Level 2. If you have mastered open-hand movements such as the chop and catching a kick, perform them very slowly in concert with your breathing. Always lead with your feet, moving slowly into the stances of your choice. Keep your balance, and never overextend your hand or foot movements. Breathe from your nose, and focus only on the technique you are performing at that moment. After a few months of practice, try the Level 2 cooldown with your eyes closed.

Level 3. After you are comfortable with Level 1 and Level 2 cooldowns, try this:

Develop your own slow motion routine by combining a variety of open hand strikes, blocks, and stances of your choice. Remain low in your stances, and move slowly and gracefully from one position to the next.

Cardio Kickboxing Intervals

Level 1. A Level 1 interval cardio kickboxing program is low in intensity. To begin, punch and kick at a pace where you can carry on a conversation, but could not say super-califragilisticexpialidoshes without taking a breath. Your work and rest intervals should be the same amount of time in the first few months of your training, anywhere from fifteen seconds each up to three minutes each. For instance, you can kick and punch for thirty seconds, and then shadowbox for thirty seconds. As your fitness increases, add time to your work periods while keeping your recovery period the same.

Perform your work period at an intensity that's just a bit higher than your steady state. (Steady state means you are moving comfortably, with slightly labored breathing.) Your recovery period (stepping in place or slow shadowboxing), should be lower in intensity than your steady state.

Be sure to use bilateral techniques (that is, alternate limbs). This allows the hand or foot that is not attacking to rest for a moment. This way, you can throw bilateral punches and kicks for a longer time without fatiguing. If you perform several unilateral movements in a row (repeated left jabs or left front kicks without a break), lactate may build up in your working muscles and limit your ability to continue.

If you are a Level 1 cardio kickboxer, don't train more than three times per week.

Level 2. Warm up for six to eight minutes. Increase your speed, height, and arousal level, but not too much. Punch and kick at seventy percent of your maximum effort for one minute, until you begin huffing and puffing. If your legs burn, you are kicking too fast. Slow down a bit in order to stay below your anaerobic threshold and to prevent deadening lactate from curtailing your workout.

After one minute of work, take a one-minute shadowbox intermission. Then do another punch/kick combination for one minute. Continue to alternate one-minute, upper-limit punching/kicking intervals with one minute of easy shadowboxing. This allows you to train at the upper limits of your aerobic capacity, thereby increasing your ability to tolerate lactate, and increasing your anaerobic threshold. Slow shadowboxing recovery intervals allow lactic acid to circulate so you are primed for your next effort. Easy shadowboxing is the best way to disperse lactic acid.

Level 3. For Level 3 cardio kickboxers, increase the speed and height of your kicks during your intervals. These "power intervals" train your heart muscle more effectively than a single bout of continuous training. During power interval training, your heart must overcome a greater resistance. This leads to improved heart rate function. Your heart empties more fully, increasing your stroke volume and cardiac output. Your body will thank your brain when you have completed your workout.

Punch and kick at ninety-five percent intensity for fifteen seconds. Then take a forty-five second slow shadowbox break to get ready for the next bout. Because your work/rest cycle is relatively short, you can repeat the cycle up to twenty times within a cardio kickboxing workout.

Perceived Exertion

A Level 3 cardio kickboxing program is very high in intensity as rated on the Perceived Exertion Scale. The Perceived Exertion Scale, or Borg Scale, is a subjective rating of your intensity from 6 (very low) to 20 (very high). Six correlates to sixty heart beats per minute, and 20 feels like a maximum heart rate of two hundred beats per minute.

You can last up to fifteen seconds at a perceived exertion of 18 during a Level 3 cardio kickboxing program (a rating of 18 is considered very difficult). Then you must recover. Use this approach only if you are very fit and athletic.

CHAPTER 10

Muscles

You have three basic types of muscle fibers: Type I, Type II-a intermediate, and Type II-b. The following sections explain the differences between these types, including what they are for and when you use them in cardio kickboxing.

Type I Muscle Fibers

Type I muscles fibers are red. They are endurance muscles, and are considered to be slow-twitch fibers. They also stabilize your posture. Your postural muscles are constantly activated while you are in an upright position in any one of the cardio kickboxing stances. These muscles also keep you balanced and upright while punching and kicking.

Type I fibers are recruited during the first few minutes of your cardio kickboxing® program. They are capable of less force but keep you punching and kicking longer than Type II fibers. Type I fibers utilize oxygen, which means they are aerobic in nature. They are smaller and contain less energy than Type II fibers, but their blood-oxygen content is high. They are the muscles that provide the endurance for you to complete your cardio kickboxing workout. Slow-twitch, Type I fibers can contract repeatedly without fatigue.

Type II-a Intermediate Muscle Fibers

Type II-a intermediate fibers are somewhat oxidative, which means they use a combination of the aerobic and glycogen systems. (Glycogen is a type of sugar used as an energy source.) These are recruited after Type I fibers. Type II-a intermediate fibers are fast-twitch with moderate endurance. They are slightly trainable. You can prepare them to be like Type II-b fast-twitch fibers, or to be like Type I endurance fibers. If you do interval punch-kick combinations, your Type II-a intermediate fibers will take on the characteristics of Type II-b fibers. Long, slow, shadowboxing, however, will move them toward the Type I fibers.

Type II-b Muscle Fibers

Type II-b fibers are white, anaerobic with a high glycogen content, and fast-twitch, which means they are more efficient at fast contraction speeds. They have few capillaries and low endurance but a high power output. They are faster, stronger, and provide more force than Type I fibers, but they fatigue quickly.

If you boast a predominant number of fast-twitch fibers, you probably are good at throwing fast, powerful kicks. Successful, competitive kickboxers possess mostly fast-twitch Type II-b muscle fibers.

You use Type I fibers during your warm-up and stance training. As you increase to fifty percent intensity on your punches and kicks, Type II-a intermediate fibers join in. And finally, when you speed up to seventy-five percent of your maximum, you fire up your Type II-b fibers.

Cardio Kickboxing® utilizes all of these fibers in a forty-five minute workout. Some of the latest research suggests that there are even more muscle fiber types on a continuum from slow-twitch to fast-twitch.

Muscle Contractions

When you throw a basic punch or kick, some muscles are contracting and others are lengthening. For example, when you execute a jab, your triceps muscles contract concentrically to extend your elbow. (A concentric contraction is a shortening of the muscle fibers between two joints.) This forces your biceps to lengthen into an eccentric contraction (a lengthening of the muscle fibers) to decelerate your jab so your elbow does not hyperextend.

When you throw a front kick, your quadriceps perform a concentric contraction. Your hamstrings eccentrically lengthen to decelerate your kick to prevent you from hyperextending your knee. When you retract your foot back to your knee, your hamstrings contract, which flexes your knee, and your quadriceps eccentrically lengthen.

Delayed Onset Muscle Soreness (DOMS)

You may experience unexplained muscle soreness from some of your more powerful cardio kickboxing techniques. Answer this question: Why are your biceps (the antagonist muscles) sore after punching drills, when your triceps (agonist) are supposed to be doing all of the work? You're correct in thinking that when you extend your elbow for a jab, your triceps contract. But your biceps decelerate the speed of your punch. When you decelerate your punches and kicks, your antagonist muscles must stop a powerful force. Look at the development of a professional boxer's back (latissimus dorsi). Some of these boxers don't lift weights but their back muscles are well developed from the constant eccentric contraction that their backs endure every time they throw a punch.

This eccentric contraction of your antagonist muscles may cause delayed onset muscle soreness (DOMS). Therefore, just like always, begin slowly, and progress gradually. Give yourself plenty of time to master cardio kickboxing techniques. Then, your antagonist muscles will adapt to your newfound power.

Activating Your Muscles

A professional kickboxer's goal is to punch and kick using as little energy as possible. In cardio kickboxing however, you want to use as much energy as possible to recruit more muscle fibers, increase your aerobic power, and burn fat.

Slow shadowboxing may recruit only half the number of muscle fibers of kicking combinations at high speed. One motor neuron may innervate (stimulate) one thousand muscle fibers in your calf while you are in an easy cat stance; another motor neuron may activate ten thousand muscle fibers in your gluteals during your powerful square stance.

Your cardio kickboxing muscles need mind-to-muscle stimulation to punch and kick. A stimulus to a motor unit contracts your muscles on an all-or-none principle. Use mental focus to activate as many muscle fibers as possible during each technique. For instance, when you throw a punch, imagine every fiber in your biceps and triceps contributing to the movement.

Power

The power in all of your punches and kicks is generated from the core muscles of your hips and abdominal area. Your core muscles include your abdominals (rectus abdominis, external, and internal obliques), hips (gluteus maximus, gluteus minimus, abductors and adductors) and the muscles in your back (quadratus lomborum and erector spinae). Be sure that you strengthen these muscles either during or after your cardio kickboxing routine.

Power is equal to force times speed. If your force is zero or your speed is zero, your power is equal to zero. But if your force is great, and your speed is awesome, the power in your punch or kick will be astounding. So in order for a punch or kick to be powerful, it must have both force and speed.

Speed is a combination of reaction time and movement time. Reaction time is measured from the moment you think about executing a technique until you actually move muscles. For example, reaction time measures from the moment you think about kicking to the moment you begin to move your leg.

Movement time is measured from the instant you move your leg to start your kick to the instant your kick is complete. Cardio kickboxing drills are tailor-made to enhance your movement time. Deliver all of your techniques as efficiently as possible, with no wasted movement.

CHAPTER 11

Home Training

Cardio Kickboxing® at home is easy and convenient. Home training helps you keep your skills sharp and, more importantly, motivates you to continue your training. A consistent program can help you cardio kickbox well into your twilight years.

Many home exercise routines are programmed for failure. Cardio Kickboxing is different. Although it may seem like "just another aerobic exercise," you can do a variety of drills depending on your needs and goals. You do not need a sparring partner to keep you going (although you might convince your spouse or your children to follow along). You can customize your home workouts to fit your mood at that moment, and take the opportunity to work on techniques that you don't get to practice as much at the gym. Put on your cross-training shoes, cue your favorite cassette tape, and rock and roll.

Preparing for Your Cardio Kickboxing Home Workout

As always, mentally prepare yourself for an explosive cardio kickboxing session.

Imagine the "feel" of an awesome workout. "See" yourself punching and kicking with perfect form. Allow no interruptions! Take the phone off of the hook and lock the doors. A full-length mirror can be helpful to check your form. Make sure that you have easy access to water.

Also, take your surroundings into account. A living room full of furniture probably isn't the best place to practice spinning jump kicks. However, front kicks and side kicks don't require a lot of room, and you can always work up a good sweat with an intense shadowboxing session.

Finally, training at home should always be performed as if you were being observed by a cardio kickboxing instructor. Maintain perfect posture, and perform all of your punches and kicks with precision. It is easy to get sloppy if no one is watching. Don't let this happen to you.

Your Home Cardio Kickboxing Workout

Step 1. Warm up for five to eight minutes. If you can, watch yourself in a mirror and let your thoughts drift to your goals.

Step 2. After the warm-up, continue shadowboxing and lightly stretch your entire body. Hold each stretch between fifteen and thirty seconds. It will help you to relax. At the same time imagine your muscles as pliable as putty.

Step 3. Perform the first cardio kickboxing drill of your choice.

Step 4. Take a thirty-second shadowboxing break, and then do another drill. Continue to alternate between work and recovery for the duration of your workout.

Step 5. Cool down with slow shadowboxing, the cooldown and stretching.

Step 6. Close your eyes and visualize having reached your cardio kickboxing goals.

Dynamic Flexibility

Home training is the perfect opportunity to improve your flexibility and your kicks. You can use a sturdy chair, stool, or wall to brace yourself, allowing you to kick higher than ever before. As your balance improves, use the chair less and less. Soon, you will be capable of throwing Level 3 kicks without a prop.

To warm up, practice slow, controlled front, side, and back leg swings. Keep both knees soft. Let your kicking leg swing gently, like a pendulum. Perform ten repetitions with each leg for each exercise.

Next, perform a leg swing, but instead of letting your leg drop, hold your leg with your free hand as high as you can for three seconds. Then let go of your leg with your hand and try to keep your leg from dropping (Figure 11-1). Attempt to hold it with leg strength alone for three seconds, then relax.

After your front, side, and back leg swings, you are ready to perform dynamic flexibility exercises for your roundhouse kick, side kick, and hook kick. I say to try ten repetitions of each exercise, but if you can't do ten, don't be discouraged. It takes time to build leg strength and flexibility, so do as many as you can. As your strength improves, add one more repetition until you reach ten. Remember, careful consistent practice is the key to success.

Figure 11-1

Tips on Home Training

- Concentrate on each punch and kick as though it's the last one you'll ever perform.

- Practice bilaterally. That is, don't just focus on one side of your body.

- Work on your least favorite punches and kicks, especially those that you might not normally practice in front of others.

- Practice to your favorite music. Stay with the beat for motivation and rhythm enhancement.

- Increase the intensity of your punches and kicks to improve your aerobic power and fitness.

- If you get tired and sloppy, slow down or take a break.

- Drink water before you begin. Sip water between combinations. Drink water after your workout.

Figure 11-2

Figure 11-3

Roundhouse Kick

Hold a stool (or chair or wall) for balance with your left hand and lift your right knee up to your side in a roundhouse kick fold position (Figure 11-2). Use your right hand to raise your knee a little higher. Let go with your hand and attempt to keep your knee up using the strength of your leg muscles. Without allowing your knee to drop, perform up to ten consecutive roundhouse kicks (Figure 11-3). Switch sides and repeat with your left leg.

Side Kick

Hold onto the stool with your left hand and lift your right knee into a side kick fold position (Figure 11-4). Use your right hand to add a few more inches of height. Then throw up to ten consecutive side kicks without allowing your knee to drop (Figure 11-5). Switch sides and repeat with your left leg.

Figure 11-4

Figure 11-5

Figure 11-6

Hook Kick

Hold onto the stool with your left hand and lift your right knee into a hook kick fold position (Figure 11-6). Use your right hand to add a few more inches of height. Then throw ten consecutive side hook kicks without allowing your knee to drop (Figure 11-7). Switch sides and repeat with your left leg.

The purpose of these dynamic stretching exercises is to strengthen the opposing muscle groups at the end ranges of motion. Imagine how much easier it will be to throw perfect kicks if your muscles are strong enough to hold your leg in position until you complete your kick. No longer must you rely on momentum to blast a kick higher. You can change the trajectory of your kicks at will, because now you have the strength to do so.

Figure 11-7

CHAPTER 12

Combinations

Combinations let you practice consecutive cardio kickboxing® techniques. They mix punching, kicking, blocking, stances, and footwork. Combinations add a new level of difficulty and intensity to your workouts and help to improve your coordination and agility.

Keep your elbows and knees slightly bent (soft) on all of your punches, kicks, strikes, and blocks.

Double Jab

Start with your left leg forward in a fighting stance. Step forward with your left foot and execute two consecutive jabs with your left hand (Figure 12-1). Switch sides and repeat.

Jab, Hook

Start with your left leg forward in a fighting stance. Step forward with your left foot and execute a jab (Figure 12-2). As soon as you retract your jab to your original fighting stance position, throw a left hook (Figure 12-3). Switch sides and repeat.

Figure 12-1

Figure 12-2

Figure 12-3

Figure 12-4

Jab, Reverse Punch

Start with your left leg forward in a fighting stance. Step forward with your left foot and simultaneously throw a left hand jab (Figure 12-4). Retract your jab and immediately throw a right reverse punch (Figure 12-5). Switch sides and repeat.

Jab, Reverse Punch, Hook

Start with your left leg forward in a fighting stance. Step forward with your left foot and simultaneously throw a left hand jab (Figure 12-6). Retract your jab and immediately throw a right reverse punch (Figure 12-7). Then immediately follow up with a left hook (Figure 12-8).

Overhead Block, Reverse Punch

Step forward with your left leg into a square stance and throw an overhead block with your left arm (Figure 12-9). At the completion of the block, immediately throw a right reverse punch and simultaneously twist your right hip and extend your right knee back into a front stance (Figure 12-10). Repeat with your other side.

Figure 12-5

Figure 12-6

Figure 12-7

Figure 12-8

Figure 12-9

Center Block, Reverse Punch

Step forward with your left leg into a square stance and execute a center block with your left arm (Figure 12-11). At the completion of the block, throw a right reverse punch and simultaneously straighten your right knee back into a front stance (Figure 12-12). Repeat with your other side.

Figure 12-10

Figure 12-11

Figure 12-12

Figure 12-13

Downward Block, Reverse Punch

Step forward with your left leg into a square stance and execute a downward block with your left arm (Figure 12-13). At the completion of the block, immediately throw a right reverse punch and simultaneously straighten your right knee back into a front stance (Figure 12-14). Repeat with your other side.

Figure 12-14

Figure 12-15

Figure 12-16

Figure 12-17

Overhead Block, Center Block, Downward Block, Reverse Punch

Step forward with your left leg into a square stance. Simultaneously throw a left overhead block (Figure 12-15). Bring your left arm across your body into a center block (Figure 12-16), then a downward block (Figure 12-17). Finally, execute a right reverse punch and retract

Figure 12-18

Figure 12-19

your left arm (Figure 12-18). Repeat. Do not be overwhelmed. Look at each part, instead of the whole.

Front Kick and Grab

Start with your left hand and left leg forward in a fighting stance. Throw a right leg front kick (Figure 12-19) and then grab with your right hand (Figure 12-20). Repeat.

Double Stepping Punch

Step forward into a front stance with your right leg. Simultaneously, throw a right arm punch high to head level (Figure 12-21). Then throw a reverse punch with your left hand to the midsection (Figure 12-22). Repeat.

Overhead Block, Downward Block, Punch

Step forward with your left leg into a square stance. Simultaneously throw a left overhead block (Figure 12-23). Then with your right arm, throw a punch to the midsection as you straighten your right knee into a front stance (Figure 12-24). Finally, throw a front punch with your left arm (Figure 12-25). Repeat.

Figure 12-20

Figure 12-21

Figure 12-22

Figure 12-23

Figure 12-24

Figure 12-25

Lean Away, Defensive Side Kick

Start with your left leg forward in a fighting position. Lean back, supporting all of your weight with your right leg (Figure 12-26). Throw a defensive side kick with your left leg (Figure 12-27). Switch sides and repeat.

Duck Under, Punch

Bend your knees and your waist while keeping your hands up in a fighting position (Figure 12-28). Stay low and twist your hips for power as you throw a hook punch (Figure 12-29).

Front Kick, Jab

Start with your left hand and left leg forward in a fighting stance. Execute a right leg front kick (Figure 12-30) and step forward.

Figure 12-26

Keep your hands up in a fighting position. When your right foot touches the floor, throw a jab with your right hand (Figure 12-31).

Figure 12-27

Figure 12-28

Figure 12-29

Figure 12-30

Jab, Punch, Roundhouse Kick

From a fighting stance throw a jab with your front hand (Figure 12-32). This creates an opening for your reverse punch (Figure 12-33). If your imaginary adversary manages to block both of these punches, snap a roundhouse kick with your back leg to the open target (Figure

Figure 12-31

Figure 12-32

Figure 12-33

Figure 12-34

12-34). Flow from one move to the next so that your imaginary opponent will have difficulty blocking all three techniques. Switch sides and repeat.

Figure 12-35

Figure 12-36

Figure 12-37

Swing Kick, Double Punch

From a fighting stance throw a rear leg swing kick to the torso of your imaginary opponent (Figure 12-35). Follow up immediately with a jab (Figure 12-36) and then reverse punch (Figure 12-37). After you throw your swing kick, lean into your punches for maximum power. Switch sides and repeat.

Punch, Punch, Kick, Punch

Start with your left leg forward in a fighting stance. Throw a right reverse punch and pivot your right foot into a front stance (Figure 12-38). Throw a left punch while remaining in your front stance (Figure 12-39). Snap a front kick with your right rear leg (Figure 12-40) and bring it back to your original stance position. Explode with a final reverse punch with your right arm (Figure 12-41). Repeat with your other side.

Figure 12-38

Figure 12-39

Figure 12-40

Figure 12-41

Backfist, Shuffle, Side Kick

Begin with your left leg forward in a fighting stance. Throw a backfist strike with your left hand (Figure 12-42). Shuffle by sliding your right foot up to your left foot (Figure 12-43). Throw a side kick with your left leg (Figure 12-44). Switch sides and repeat.

Figure 12-42

Figure 12-43

Figure 12-44

Figure 12-45

Karate Chop, Side Kick

Start with your left leg forward in a fighting stance. Chop with your right hand (Figure 12-45). Pivot on your front foot and throw a side kick with your back leg (Figure 12-46). Switch sides and repeat.

Figure 12-46

Figure 12-47

Figure 12-48

Figure 12-49

Reverse Punch, Side Kick, Reverse Punch

Start with your left leg forward in a fighting stance. Throw a right reverse punch (Figure 12-47). Without a pause, throw a right leg side kick (Figure 12-48). Drop into a front stance with your kicking leg forward and finish with a powerful left reverse punch (Figure 12-49). Switch sides and repeat.

Figure 12-50

Figure 12-51

Front Kick, Side Kick

Start with your left leg forward in a fighting stance. Throw a rear leg front kick (Figure 12-50). As soon as your right foot makes contact with the floor, begin your side kick (Figure 12-51). Go for speed, power and, smoothness. Switch sides and repeat.

Once you are comfortable with these combinations, feel free to create your own. Combine blocks, punches, kicks, and footwork in a display of agility and power. Whenever practicing combinations, be sure you have enough space to not run into anyone else. Don't let your arms and legs flail uncontrollably.

Beginners should concentrate on correct form. Experienced cardio kickboxers can go for power and speed. Have fun!

CHAPTER 13

Special Drills

This chapter presents a series of special drills you can do for a change of pace in your workouts. It also includes special exercises to improve upper body, strength, and leg strength.

Modeling

This drill involves at least two people. One person is the instructor, and the other person must imitate every movement the instructor makes. The goal is to virtually beat the instructor to the punch. Modeling requires observation and anticipation. The student should follow the instructor's movements below. Be sure to warm up for five to eight minutes before beginning.

Step 1. The instructor assumes a left foot forward fighting position (Figure 13-1).

Step 2. The instructor moves lightly on the balls of his/her feet.

Step 3. The instructor explodes with a right reverse punch (Figure 13-2) and then recovers.

Figure 13-1

Figure 13-2

Figure 13-3   Figure 13-4

Step 4. The instructor fires a left leg defensive side kick, and then recovers.

Step 5. The instructor switches sides and repeats the entire routine.

Kiai Drill

Throughout your workout, kiai with a punch or kick. A kiai is a yell from your diaphragm. The purpose of your kiai is to energize your attack. Your kiai also helps you to contract your torso muscles in case your imaginary opponent strikes at the same moment you do.

Self-Defense Combinations

Self-defense combinations in your cardio kickboxing® routine add realism to your strikes and attacks. Develop a special "self-defense workout" requiring that only valid self-defense strategies can be used for your training during that session. Be sure to warm up for five to eight minutes before beginning. Self-defense techniques include:

1. Low front kicks, side kicks, and roundhouse kicks (Figure 13-3).
2. Knee strikes and elbow strikes.
3. Palm heel, spear hand, and forearm strikes (Figure 13-4).

Olympic Cardio Kickboxing

In the 2000 Olympics, the sport of taekwondo will be a medal sport for the first time. To celebrate this event, enjoy a special "Olympic Taekwondo" training session. The rules are as follows:

1. Perform three three-minute rounds with one minute of active rest between each round.

2. The rounds must consist of high-intensity punching, kicking, and blocking to the proper target areas. You are required to kick above the belt and punch only to the body of your imaginary opponent.

3. Between each round, there will be a one-minute active rest period. Active rest is simply marching in place with your eyes closed. During active rest, you will mentally prepare for your next round of fighting.

4. After your third three-minute round, depending on your physical condition, you can choose to cool down or finish your cardio kickboxing routine with some Level 1 drills.

Figure 13-5

Bodywork

1. Begin in your fighting position.
2. Imagine your opponent punching to your body.
3. Exhale and contract your abdominal muscles on each imaginary punch.

Uppercuts with Speed

1. Imagine your opponent in front of you.
2. Assume a horse stance with your hands in fighting position.
3. Throw ten consecutive uppercuts, alternating hands. Rest ten seconds. This counts as one cycle. Repeat another five cycles (Figure 13-5).
4. Switch stances and repeat six cycles with your right leg forward, then the left leg forward.

Wrist and Shoulder Alignment Exercise

1. Assume a push-up position on your first two knuckles on a mat or carpeted floor.
2. Keep your hands shoulder width apart.
3. Keep your back straight and your neck neutral (Figure 13-6). If you cannot hold this position from your feet, try it from your knees.
4. Hold this position for five seconds. Rest five seconds, then repeat.
5. When you can hold this position easily for five cycles, try knuckle push-ups.

Figure 13-6

Figure 13-7

Knuckle Push-ups

1. Assume a push-up position.
2. Close your fists so that the knuckles of your index finger and middle finger are pressed against the floor.
3. Keep your back straight and your neck neutral.
4. Slowly flex your elbows so that your chest comes within an inch from the floor (Figure 13-7).
5. Extend your elbows until they are half an inch from full extension. Do not lock your elbows.
6. Continue your push-ups until you begin to lose perfect body alignment.
7. Rest fifteen seconds and then perform another set.

Figure 13-8

Kicking the Length of the Floor

Be sure to warm up for five to eight minutes before beginning.
1. Begin in your left foot forward fighting stance.
2. Execute a right leg front kick and step forward with that same leg (Figure 13-8).
3. Now that your right leg is forward, throw a left rear leg front kick.

Figure 13-9

Figure 13-10

4. Repeat this sequence for front kicks, roundhouse kicks, and side kicks all the way down the floor and back.

Circle Drill

Be sure to warm up for five to eight minutes before beginning.
1. Form a circle with all students facing the center.
2. Begin in a left foot forward fighting position.
3. Call out your favorite kick, punch, or combination.
3. Lead the entire group through ten repetitions on each side.
4. Next, the person to your right calls out his/her favorite technique, and he/she leads the group through ten reps.
5. Continue until all the students have had a chance to call out and lead the rest of the class through their favorite techniques.

Hand Techniques

Be sure to warm up for five to eight minutes before beginning.
1. Perform a front hand jab on the count of "one" (Figure 13-9). Switch sides and repeat.
2. Perform a rear hand reverse punch on the count of "two." Switch sides and repeat.
3. On the count of "three" throw a front hand hook (Figure 13-10). Switch sides and repeat.
4. Next, call out a number. If you call out "one," throw a front hand jab.
5. If you call out "two" throw a rear hand reverse punch.
6. If you call out "three" throw a front hand hook.

7. You may combine your punches by calling "one-two" for jab-punch or "one-two-three" for jab, punch, hook.

Foot Techniques

Be sure to warm up for five to eight minutes before beginning.

1. Perform a rear leg front kick on the count of "one." Switch sides and repeat.
2. On the count of "two" throw a rear leg roundhouse kick. Switch sides and repeat.
3. On the count of "three" throw a rear leg side kick. Switch sides and repeat.
4. On the count of "four" throw a rear leg swing kick. Switch sides and repeat.
5. Next call out a number at random.
6. Do this drill until you have thrown all four kicks with both legs at least once.

Figure 13-11

Plyometrics

Plyometrics consists of a variety of bounding drills that increase your power. The bounding action takes advantage of the stretch-recoil and stretch-reflex properties of your muscles. The quick stretch applied to the muscle during push-off is thought to increase muscle contraction, enhancing explosiveness.

Warm up thoroughly before you start plyometrics. When you begin plyometric training, jump no more than two inches from the floor. Take at least a minute between plyometric sets to let your heart rate settle down. Perform just one set of each exercise. Because of joint stress, perform plyometrics a maximum of once a week.

Set 1—Front Stance Jumps. Begin in a left front stance. Jump up and switch your legs in the air so that you land in a right front stance. Repeat nine more times. Take no rest between jumps.

Set 2—Jump Kick Fold. Raise your right knee quickly so that your whole body leaves the floor (Figure 13-11). Let your left leg follow your right leg as you are airborne (similar to a jump kick). Fall softly to the floor, rolling from the balls of your feet to your heels. Repeat, beginning with your left leg. Perform ten consecutive jumps, alternating each leg.

Set 3—Running Step Jump. Take a three-step running start and bound off both feet, throwing your arms in the air (like Superman jumping out a window) (Figure 13-12). After landing, take three steps back and continue nine more times.

Set 4—Evade the Sweep. Begin with your feet a little less than shoulder-width apart. Jump up and pull your heels toward your buttocks (Figure 13-13) and land solidly in your original position. Do ten repetitions.

Figure 13-12

Figure 13-13

Figure 13-14

Figure 13-15

Set 5—Awaken the Tiger. Touch your fingers to the floor (Figure 13-14) and bound up as high as you can (Figure 13-15). Do ten repetitions. Bend from your knees. Keep your back neutral.

Sticking Hands

1. Get a partner and face each other in a fighting position.
2. Keep your elbows close to your body and hold your hands up as if to block an attack.
3. With your right hand, make light, continuous contact with your partner's left hand, and with your left hand make contact with your partner's right hand.
4. "Attack" your partner gently; that is, push slowly and gently toward your partner's chest.
5. Your partner, feeling the movement, should redirect the "attack" without any muscular tension.
6. Allow your partner to attack as you defend.
7. Finally, both of you can attack and defend at will without tension, speed, or force.
8. Try it with your eyes closed. Feel the attack and redirect. Counter when ready. Flow.

Cool Down

Always complete your cardio kickboxing training with a cooldown and stretching. Cooling down is simply slowing down. Decrease your intensity and speed.

Stretching during the final moments of your cardio kickboxing workout is imperative. Your muscles are warm. This is the time to improve your flexibility.

CHAPTER 14

Bag Work and Pads

In the first few months of cardio kickboxing® training, perfect your punching and kicking form. Your primary training aid should be a mirror. Later, you may decide to add intensity by punching and kicking a bag or target pad. These devices allow you to add speed and power to all of your techniques.

However, if your wrists are not firm and your toes are not pulled back you will feel it, and possibly injure yourself. So at first, hit softly, and like always, gradually progress to increased power.

Bag Work

Warm up before striking the bag. Begin slowly! Relax and focus. Maintain proper form. Launch your movements from the ground up. When you punch, use hand wraps and bag gloves (Figure 14-1). Make sure that the point of impact for punches is your first two knuckles. For kicks, make contact with the top of your foot, the ball of your foot, your heel, or the side of your foot.

At first, perform single techniques. After you have practiced jabs, reverse punches, hooks, front kicks, roundhouse kicks, and side kicks, perform your combinations exactly as you would use them in cardio kickboxing. Keep your hands up, stay light on your feet, and imagine the bag as your opponent. Cool down by slowly shadowboxing the bag. Conclude with stretching.

Target Pad Training

Target pads can help sharpen your punches and kicks. Warm up and stretch before using the pads. Go slowly at first. Touch the pad with each strike (Figure 14-2). After a thorough warm-up, snap your kicks and punches, but not too hard. Remember, never fully extend your knees. Retract your foot as quickly as you threw it. Hit with the appropriate part of your foot (Figure 14-3).

Figure 14-1

Figure 14-2

Figure 14-3

Your partner can hold a pad in each hand, providing you with moving targets. (Be sure never to hold the pads in front of your face, for obvious reasons.) Each time your partner moves the pads, execute a different kick or punch. For example, if the target is facing down, do a front kick. If it is down at a forty-five degree angle, throw a roundhouse kick. If it is perpendicular to the floor, shoot a side kick. Throw your punches and kicks from your fighting position. Watch your partner's solar plexus and see the pads peripherally. Punch and kick with perfect form and enjoy the feeling of contact.

CHAPTER 15

Cardio Kickboxing for Life

This chapter offers some general strategies to keep you training for life. It also includes cross-training tips and discusses what to look for in a good cardio kickboxing instructor.

Cardio Kickboxing: Anytime, Anywhere

Cardio kickboxing can be practiced in a gym, hotel room, bus station, or airport. I have practiced cardio kickboxing in all of these venues. Sure I received some quizzical glances, but so what? I use my headphones to spur me on, and I get a great workout on otherwise sedentary trips.

Cardio Kickboxing on the Road

A friend of mine loaned me a bus pass for a month. I could travel anywhere within the forty-eight contiguous states. I wasted no time. I traveled from Dallas to California, back to Dallas, to Pennsylvania, and then back to Dallas.

During each stop, while my fellow travelers got some food, I found a corner of a restaurant or bus station, turned up my headphones and cardio kickboxed. I carried a towel in my duffel bag so that after each mini-cardio kickboxing workout I could dry off.

These mini-workouts (ten to twenty minutes long) were short but intense. I began with a slow shadowboxing warm-up, followed by thirty seconds of easy stretching. Then I blasted into high-speed punches and low kicks. Gradually, I increased the intensity of my kicks until within five minutes I was kicking high and fast. It was exhilarating. I exploded against my imaginary opponent to the beat of music that nobody else could hear.

Within minutes, I was punching and kicking fast, high and with power. Since I knew each cardio kickboxing workout would be very short, it was easy to give one hundred percent. During the last two minutes of each mini-workout, I cooled down by gradually bringing my kicks down to waist and knee level. I finished with some light stretching.

Those mini-cardio kickboxing breaks were truly invigorating. I cannot imagine having traveled the country without those invigorating interludes. After each workout, I purchased a snack and carried it on the bus. For the next couple of hours, I feasted on my cardio kickboxing endorphin high.

Cardio Kickboxing in Hotels

I do a lot of traveling. Some hotels have gyms, others don't. Regardless, I always spend a few minutes cardio kickboxing in my hotel room.

All it takes is the music from the radio-alarm (or a music-television station) and the hotel room mirror. A mirror provides you with immediate feedback about your punching and kicking form, speed, and intensity.

I begin with an easy warm-up. And since there is always a wall close by, I use it for the dynamic flexibility exercises discussed in Chapter 11.

These slow-motion strength-kicks are a terrific warm-up. I follow them with punch-kick combinations. During combinations, I scrutinize my form in the mirror. Is my back straight? Did I telegraph the kick? Would it have worked in a fighting situation?

After about twenty minutes of combinations, it's time to cool down and stretch. I usually do my stretching on the bed, as it is large enough to perform front and side splits.

Cardio Kickboxing on a Plane

I know what you're thinking. No, you are not punching and kicking up and down the aisle. Instead, crank up your headphones (after the pilot informs you it's okay to use electronic devices), and *imagine* your cardio kickboxing workout. Sport psychology studies show that if you think about throwing a punch or kick, you can actually enhance the nerve-to-muscle function, so that when you actually throw your punches and kicks, they will be faster, higher, and more powerful.

Visualize your techniques as clearly as you can. Always imagine you are executing with perfect form. Use as many senses as possible. Allow your imaginary punches and kicks to flow to the beat of your music. "Feel" your punches and kicks extend and retract as if you were actually performing your cardio kickboxing workout. And when you have completed your imaginary cooldown, feel refreshed, alert, and ready.

Cardio Kickboxing When You're Injured

Cardio kickboxing is a full-body workout. But if you have injured an arm, you can perform your kicks. If one of your legs is sore, throw punches. It is easy to reach your target heart rate doing kicks, but it is equally effective using your upper body, if you maintain a high intensity.

Be careful not to overtrain, as your balance may be disturbed by your injury. Check with your physician if you have a strain or sprain that persists for longer than a week. Don't perform any exercises that will aggravate your injury.

Cardio Kickboxing When You're Bored

For a change of pace, turn up your tunes and shadowbox. Let your mind wander. Dissociate. Let your attention drift. Or, think about an unsolved problem. Who knows, you may come up with a solution. Although dissociation is a nice change of pace, don't make it a habit. Dissociation is a lazy form of meditation.

Cardio Kickboxing When You're Tired

There will be times when you're not in the mood to train, but you know you should. Crank up your music. Drink some water. If you haven't eaten in a couple of hours, have a snack. Then convince yourself to warm up. If you don't feel like completing your entire cardio kickboxing workout, that's okay, but at least warm up. After you warm up, call it a day if you're still tired. Nine times out of ten, your warm-up will inspire you to complete your cardio kickboxing workout.

Marathon Cardio Kickboxing

When I was in college, I was trying to figure out a way to earn some gas money so I could drive down to Texas from Pennsylvania. A friend of mine suggested we sell tickets to a "karate marathon." His part was easy; all he had to do was sell tickets. I was the one who had to fight seven guys in a row for three, three-minute rounds. After it was over, I was physically ill for three days. But at the moment, it was a peak experience. We had music blaring which kept us pumped up. Music has always motivated me to peak performance.

To train for a "cardio kickboxing marathon" begin with a twenty-minute workout. Add two minutes a week until you are throwing combinations for fifty minutes straight. Don't forget your five-minute warm-up and five-minute cooldown.

Going for Perfection

Your cardio kickboxing workout will maximize your endurance and flexibility, but if you want to improve your strength and muscle size, weight training is your answer. Train each muscle group twice a week, and if possible, lift weights on the days that you are not cardio kickboxing.

To improve your cardio kickboxing footwork, jump rope. Jumping rope keeps you light on your feet and improves your muscular endurance. When you do not have a rope, try footwork drills. Practice your shuffles, steps, push-slides, and switches.

To punch and kick faster, improve the efficiency of your technique by perfecting your form. Employ the services of a martial arts instructor to fine-tune your moves. Use a mirror to compare your form with the photos presented in this book.

To flow from one technique to the next more smoothly, and to perform multiple combinations with ease, try these strategies:

- Remain relaxed. When you try too hard, you tense your muscles.
- Focus on one thing at a time (for instance, bent knee, speed, timing, angle of foot, or target area). Trying to think about more than one item at a time will confuse your coordination.
- Slow down. If you try to move too fast when a technique is not well-learned, it will appear jerky.
- Compete only against yourself. If you are training with others, punch and kick at *your* pace. This is *your* workout.

Cardio kickboxing agility and balance may be improved by practicing the following drills:

- Always keep your supporting knee slightly bent on all kicks.
- Practice slow punches and kicks with your eyes closed.
- Attempt to throw more than a single kick consecutively (for example, double roundhouse kicks with the same leg) while remaining balanced on your other leg.
- Practice throwing your kicks in slow motion so that your stabilizer muscles must work overtime to maintain balance.

To throw your techniques with focus and purpose, try the following:

- Imagine attacking an opponent every time you punch and kick.
- Strike your imaginary opponent with the correct contact surface (for instance, first two knuckles for a punch).
- Focus your eyes on the solar plexus of your imaginary opponent.
- Relax. Contract your muscles only at the completion of your punch or kick. This increases the speed, force, and power of your technique.

Looking the Part

One way to appear as if you have spent time in the ring is to pay attention to professional boxers and kickboxers. Watch them fight. Notice their relaxed countenance. Observe how they carry themselves. If you are viewing them on television, get off of your easy chair and follow along. Punch, kick, and block. Imagine blocking their kicks. Slip their punches. Then practice in a mirror. Model your favorite fighters. Make their techniques your own.

The Gaze

After watching hundreds of cardio kickboxers, I can generally spot a novice, even though he or she may have good technique. The novice stares wide-eyed into the mirror. If this is your habit, soften your eyes. Rather than stare unblinkingly, relax your gaze. Focus on your imaginary opponent, without allowing your eyes to telegraph your intentions.

Troubleshooting Common Mistakes

The most common mistakes I have witnessed in cardio kickboxing are:

- Warming up too fast.
- Forgetting to stretch.
- Letting your elbows telegraph your punches by flinging them away from your body prior to extension.
- Muscling your punches. That is, pushing your punches instead of throwing them.
- Throwing high-intensity combinations early in the workout.
- Hyperextending elbows and knees.
- Attempting to kick too high, causing your spine to go out of neutral alignment.
- Throwing more than ten consecutive unilateral kicks.
- Kicking to your intended imaginary opponent with the wrong part of your foot.
- Too short of a recovery period between high-intensity intervals.
- Failure to retract your punch or kick at the same trajectory, and at the same speed, that you extended it.

Group Cardio Kickboxing

You can practice cardio kickboxing by yourself, with a friend, or in a group setting under the watchful eye of a cardio kickboxing instructor. If you go to a gym and take a cardio kickboxing class, be sure that your instructor is certified. But certification does not guarantee that your instructor will follow safe and effective guidelines. If your instructor forces you into complicated choreography or explosive, contra-indicated movements, it's time to find another instructor.

How to Spot a Good Instructor

A good cardio kickboxing instructor can make a big difference to your training. The popularity of cardio kickboxing means you have a choice in instructors. Take advantage of that choice and find an instructor whose personality and teaching style is right for you.

In my opinion, a good instructor should have the following qualities:
- Sees every individual in class.
- Monitors your heart rate and/or perceived exertion periodically throughout your workout.
- Is a good role model.
- Can demonstrate exemplary form for your punches and kicks.
- Is a good motivator.
- Provides you with feedback concerning your performance.
- Is not afraid to curtail his/her workout to help correct your form or answer questions during a class.
- Is concerned with your workout, not his/hers.
- Adjusts intensity according to the needs of the class.
- Shows you how to move to the slow, medium, or fast beat depending on your level.
- Will provide a few minutes before and after class to help you with your technique.

A qualified instructor should be certified. A variety of certification organizations exist, so I recommend that you call Exercise Etc. at (800) 244-1344 for information about certification programs.

Moving to the Music

Choreographing your techniques with music can link your cardio kickboxing drills together smoothly. Use the following choreographic methods and styles to help as guides. Combine two or more cardio kickboxing drills with one song. Feel free to create your own choreographic methods.

Freestyle Technique

Start with a basic punch or kick and add or subtract another punch or kick to make your workout more interesting. For example, first throw a front leg side kick ten times. Then throw ten reverse punches. Now throw ten side kick/reverse punch combinations. You can move from one combination to the next, varying the speed, intensity and stances. The freestyle technique lets you practice and refine your combinations without worry of complicated choreography.

Chorus/Verse Method

Most songs are made up of choruses and verses. The chorus is the section that repeats itself over and over again. Generally, songs alternate between verse and chorus. To use this method, simply select two different punches or kicks and alternate them with the chorus and verse. Just choose a song and you're ready to go! For instance, on the verse do a rear leg front kick. On the chorus, perform a front hand jab.

Repeat this until the song is over. It's a good idea to do a punching drill on the chorus and kicking drill on the verse for variety and to work more muscles.

Discipline

These days, master instructors and training partners are in demand, and with good reason. Your master instructor motivates you to get through that last interval of punching and kicking. Your training partner can keep your spirits up. A partner encourages you and gives you inspiration when you feel weak and tired. A partner can also help get you to the gym when you'd rather be a couch potato.

But even if you have the best instructor or most reliable workout partner, you won't get far in cardio kickboxing if you lack self-discipline. Teamwork is fine, but you've got to be motivated on your own if you're going to be your best. The search for improvement starts from within. Disciplined training is a path to a new sense of self.

> ### Do's and Don'ts of Cardio Kickboxing
>
> - Don't cardio kickbox at a high intensity every day.
> - Don't cardio kickbox from a videotape that uses hard or dangerous moves.
> - Don't cardio kickbox if you get so tired you begin to lose your form. Sloppy cardio kickboxing techniques lead to injury. If you feel yourself getting sloppy, try slow shadowboxing or walking in place.
> - Don't cardio kickbox without your physician's approval if you have any orthopedic injuries, diabetes, chronic obstructive pulmonary disease, or are over 45 years old.
> - Do cardio kickbox at least twice a week for maximum results.
> - Do monitor your body for weakness or injury.
> - Do spend time outside of cardio kickboxing working on your weaknesses (for instance, flexibility, or strength).
> - Do enjoy your workout!

Elite athletes discipline both their bodies and minds. Athletes spend hours alone with their thoughts. Periodically they examine their choices. They determine if they are training just to reach someone else's goal. They search within themselves to discover the reasons they do what they do.

Look back on your life. List your accomplishments. Any worthwhile achievement required perseverance. Finishing school, playing a musical instrument, or hauling hay demanded discipline. Draw upon your past challenges to shape your future. Holding square, front, and cat stances is a foundation for cardio kickboxing, just like doing homework was a foundation for success in school. If you develop discipline in one thing, you can train yourself for many things.

When your mind is ready your body will follow. Lao Tsu said, "Building your body can be achieved only when your mind has been disciplined." Get hooked on disciplined training. At first, it is easier to forego exercise and watch television, but an evening of lounging can't beat a spirited workout. Some people crave alcohol or gambling, but physical training is better than any drug. The secret is to convince yourself that exercise is play.

To improve your self-discipline, set guidelines as to how much time to devote to training. Set aside just a few minutes every day, or every other day. Maintain your program until it is routine. Always look forward to your activity. Never burn out. If priorities conflict, be flexible. Once training is a habit, it's easy.

Begin with baby steps. Progress gradually. In six months you will become accustomed to your training program. Increase your intensity no more than five percent for a given workout. If you are too vigorous your body will revolt. With proper planning however, you can discipline yourself to do almost anything.

Schedule

In order to train effectively, you must be realistic about how much time you have to devote to your practice. Then, allocate time to hone your strengths and fortify your weaknesses. Initially, you may discover that you don't have enough time for your practice and training. Here's where your modifications begin. Either redefine your goal or adjust your schedule.

Each of your strengths and weaknesses can be improved through a series of drills or exercises. This is true of both mind and body skills. In fact, while your body is resting, your mind can be propelling you forward using visualization or focus training.

As your training continues, you will need to make some changes depending on your progress. It is important to adjust your schedule accordingly. Your skill level will change and your strengths and weaknesses will become more balanced. Readjust. Keep a written record of your training, schedules, and evaluations. This way you can revisit your training program and change it accordingly.

CHAPTER 16

Injury Prevention and Injury Treatment

With proper training and instruction (and a little common sense), cardio kickboxing® can be one of the safest fitness programs you'll ever enjoy. Cardio kickboxing can improve your flexibility, balance, and strength, all of which are essential for life-long fitness.

However, as in any exercise program, you do run the risk of injury. The best way to reduce that risk is to understand potential trouble spots and be aware of how injuries occur. This chapter focuses on injury prevention, and will help you to increase your body awareness to prevent mishap. This chapter also presents recovery strategies to help you come back stronger than before from strains, pulls, and other common injuries. In most cases, you will stay injury-free if you maintain proper body alignment and don't exceed your abilities (for example, attempting repetitive single-leg kicks on your first day of class).

Remember, if you do suffer an injury, be sure to consult your physician.

Injuries and Treatments

Elbows. Tennis elbow can affect you even though you are a cardio kickboxer, not a tennis player. This injury, termed lateral epicondylitis, is an overuse injury of the tendon that attaches the extensor muscles in your forearm to the elbow at its bony outer knob, the lateral epicondyle.

With repeated stress from punching, striking, and blocking, the tendon can suffer microtears that cause the elbow to become tender and inflamed. Your first preventive measure is to keep your elbow "soft" at all times. That is, be sure not to lock your elbow on any punch, strike, or block.

Your second preventive measure is not to cause pain. If any strike, punch or block causes pain, modify it by changing the range of motion. Redo the speed and force of your technique. Listen to your body. Pain is your body's way of saying, "Rest me!"

If you do experience elbow pain, anti-inflammatory medicine is recommended, and so is ice. Ice your elbow for ten to twenty minutes after each cardio kickboxing session. You can also gently massage your elbow before and after a workout. Some patients receive steroid injections. Tennis elbow is slow in healing, sometimes taking from eight weeks to a year to fully recover.

Shoulders. Your shoulder has the greatest range of motion of any joint in your body. No other joint is as flexible—and unstable—as the shoulder.

The shoulder joint is a shallow ball-and-socket joint that allows your arm to move freely in all directions to block and strike. Your rotator cuff muscles hold that ball in its socket when you cock your arm to throw a chop, and when you follow through on your punches. Your shoulder depends greatly on the surrounding muscles to provide necessary stability.

A fluid-filled bursae sac acts as a shock absorber for your shoulder joint. If it is inflamed it bulges and becomes, thick, scarred, and painful. This is your body's way of letting you know that you should discontinue the cardio kickboxing techniques that created inflammation in the first place.

The shoulder area is a notorious spot for many athletic injuries. The shoulder area includes the rotator cuff muscles—supraspinatis, infraspinatus, teres minor and subscapularis—which are responsible for a variety of arm movements. However, these muscles are often largely ignored. Even if you work out every day, chances are you're not working out your rotator cuff muscles.

The rotator cuff muscles are crucial in cardio kickboxing. Although it does not take enormous strength to throw a punch, conditioning and endurance are necessary. Be sure to warm up and stretch these muscles before each cardio kickboxing session, and strengthen them afterwards by internal and external rotating exercises. Ask any fitness trainer or boxing instructor to demonstrate these exercises to you. I also recommend the UBC machine, which utilizes an upper-body cycling motion, and the shoulder alignment exercises in Chapter 13.

Knees. Several muscles extend your knee. Your quadriceps allow you to extend your leg for a full-force front kick. Your extensor muscles (rectus femoris, vastus lateralis, vastus medialis, and vastus intermedius) are on the front of your thigh. The only one of these muscles that crosses your hip is your rectus femoris.

Your hamstrings, in the back of your upper leg, generate knee flexion and hip extension. They help you retract your front, side, roundhouse, and hook kicks. These muscles are generally weaker than your quadriceps. If your hamstrings are weaker than your quadriceps, you may have a muscle imbalance that could precipitate knee problems.

On the inside of your knee closest to your groin, you have muscles called adductors. These muscles (adductor magnus, longus, brevis, and gracilis) help to pull your leg toward your body when you cock your kicks into a fold position. On the outside of your knee you have abductors. These muscles (tensor facia latae, gluteus medius) pull your leg away from your body when you perform roundhouse, side, and hook kicks. Your adductors and abductors help to stabilize your movements when you flex and extend your knees from a standing position.

There a variety of known and unknown causes of knee pain, including muscle strains and pulls, as well as ligament and cartilage injury.

Pain on the back of the inside of your knees may be bursitis. Bursitis is irritation of the bursae sac in your knee. Three muscles, your sartorius, gracilus, and semitendinosis, meet at the pes anserine. Inflammation occurs at this site if these muscles rub against one another during ax kicks and crescent kicks. Bursitis may also be caused by prolonged kicking with full knee extension. Remember to always keep your knees soft.

Ligament damage is another cause of knee pain. Your anterior cruciate ligament (ACL) may be injured by getting stuck in a rotation as you twist for your roundhouse kicks.

Your posterior cruciate ligament (PCL) may be damaged if you hyperextend your knee on a forceful front kick. A PCL strain is usually accompanied by medial collateral ligament (MCL) or ACL strain.

Pain on the outside of your knee during cardio kickboxing may be aggravated by friction on your iliotibial band. Stretching, anti-inflammatory medicine, and ice may help.

Pain behind your kneecap may be chondromalacia, a progressive softening of your patellar cartilage. Strengthen the quadriceps muscle on the inside of your knees by using a leg extension machine.

If you hold low stances, or don't warm up properly you may develop patellar tendinitis. Patellar tendinitis may also be caused by performing too many jump kicks. Ice your patellar tendon for five minutes, massage it for five minutes, and then repeat this sequence.

Within your knee joint is cartilage that protects the ends of the thigh bone (femur) and tibia. When you step down, you squish fluid out of cartilage. When you relax, fluid rushes back in. As you age, your cartilage does not absorb as much water. It dries out. You may have a cartilage problem if you feel pain, hear a clicking sound when you move the knee, or feel your knee lock.

See a doctor or sports medicine specialist if you think you have cartilage damage. Your doctor will probably ask for a more detailed history about the origin of your pain, and may also perform an arthrogram or arthroscopy to get a clearer picture of the reason for your distress.

Ankles. Ankles are the achilles heel of cardio kickboxers. An ankle sprain is generally a stretch or tear to a ligament. It may be a mild tear, a moderate tear, or a severe tear. Most sprains involve an injury to the ligaments on the outside of your ankle when your foot turns over. This is called an inversion sprain.

When your ligaments tear, they bleed. This immediate bleeding increases inflammation, which begins the extensive swelling that occurs. Swelling is the body's way of cleaning up. The fluid is channeled through the lymphatic system. As the swelling subsides, you may notice a bruise. This is blood that is close to the skin. Sometimes, the degree of bruising is an indication of how badly the ligaments were torn.

Ankle problems do not necessarily require you to curtail your cardio kickboxing. Each case depends on the severity of the specific injury. You can return to cardio kickboxing if you have a pain-free normal range of motion (that is, if you can move your ankle in all directions without pain). And be sure you can walk, jog, shuffle, and hop before you consider hardcore training.

If you injure your ankle during cardio kickboxing answer the following questions:
- Did your ankle invert?
- Could you stand up on it after the injury?
- Have you hurt this same ankle in the past?

If you answer "yes" to all of these questions, you may want to see a doctor for the injury. Your doctor's job is to determine what he or she must do to insure that the torn ligaments will repair themselves. This sometimes requires a cast. Anti-inflammatory medication may also help. Some doctors recommend bracing until your ligaments heal.

A slow-healing sprain may not be a sprain at all. Often a slight fracture can cause less swelling than a sprain. An x-ray may help determine if you indeed have a fracture.

R.I.C.E. If you experience a minor ankle injury, R.I.C.E is the cure.

R is for rest. Rest your ankle until you can walk without a limp.

I is for ice. Icing your ankle will relieve pain and reduce swelling. To ice your ankle, you can wrap ice cubes in a dishtowel and then drape the towel over the injured area. Ice your ankle for twenty minutes every two hours.

If you don't want to deal with melting ice cubes, there are also chemical icepacks that you can get at most sporting goods stores. However, some of the chemical icings are too cold and can actually blister your skin. You can also pull a bag of frozen peas out of your freezer. Vegetable bags conform to the natural curve of your ankle. When your peas thaw out, grab a bag of corn.

C is for compression. Compression, or a specially designed pressure wrap, helps to decrease the swelling. Be sure to loosen an elastic wrap before you go to sleep. Physical therapists use a special machine called JOBST that sequentially squeezes the fluid from your foot and ankle.

E is for elevation. To reduce swelling, hold your leg above your heart. A simple way to do this is to lie down and place one or two pillows under your injured ankle. You can elevate your ankle while you ice it, and at night while you sleep.

When you return to cardio kickboxing after an ankle injury, practice balancing drills before you jump into your regular workout. Unused muscle and ligaments atrophy during your time away from cardio kickboxing.

Regaining your proprioception is your first priority to prevent another ankle injury. Proprioception is your ability to balance yourself. Simple exercises help your muscles and ligaments to stimulate nerve endings that were dormant during your recuperation. For example, stand on one foot while you perform your quadriceps stretch. Switch legs and repeat. Repeat these exercises again with your eyes closed.

Stress Fractures. A sharp, focused area of pain on the bone of your lower leg might indicate a stress fracture. Pain along the entire shin might be medial tibial stress syndrome, also known as shin splints. If your leg is pain-free at rest, but hurts when you cardio kickbox, or walk up and down stairs, you might have a stress fracture. Find a tuning fork and try this test: Pass a vibrating tuning fork along your tibia. If you feel a sharp pain, that indicates the possibility of a stress fracture at that site.

Stress fractures are caused by repeatedly overloading your tibia or increasing your intensity. Take a look at your shoes. If they are more than six months old, and you train daily, they may have lost some resiliency.

Limiting impact is the first step to curing your stress fracture. Replace high-impact plyometrics and cardio kickboxing with shadowboxing and Tai Chi. If your injury is severe, a splint may be required. If you believe you are suffering from a stress fracture, consult your physician.

Osteoarthritis. If you have pain in your joints when you cardio kickbox, check with your doctor to find out if you have osteoarthritis. Osteoarthritis is a progressive, irreversible degeneration of the articular surfaces of the joints.

For example, you might feel pain on the inside, outside, or middle of your knee. It can be localized or spread out. If your knees usually hurt when you cardio kickbox, and they progressively get worse by the end of the day, you have symptoms of osteoarthritis.

Try cardio kickboxing in a warm swimming pool. Practice your punches, kicks, strikes, and blocks against the resistance of the water. Do your forms in chest-deep water. Any low-impact activity is good. Avoid going up and down stairs and squatting.

If you are overweight, losing body fat can help take the load off of your joints. Your cardio kickboxing should resemble Tai Chi in intensity if you are overweight. Keep your intensity level below the level of pain. Be sure to exercise regularly. Follow an eating plan that keeps your body fat levels low to keep the stress off of your joints.

Hyperextension. When you throw punches hard and fast, you risk hyperextending your elbow. Hyperextension causes an injury known as a stinger. The stinger can send shooting pains up your elbow and arm, and if you snap your elbow hard enough, you may chip the bone. Avoid this injury by extending your arms only ninety to ninety-five percent when punching. Never fully straighten your arms. The same also goes for your knees, which are also vulnerable to hyperextension via kicks.

Stretch for Safety

Throughout this book I've emphasized the importance of stretching. Lithe, limber muscles are less susceptible to strain and injury, and you know the importance of stretching both before and after your workouts. However, you don't need to restrict your stretches to the gym. There are many opportunities to stretch throughout the day—just after you wake up, during lunch or a coffee break, in the evening in front of the television, or just before bed.

For instance, if you find yourself sitting in the same position for long periods of time, try a stretch. Stretch your lower back (quadratus laborum, erector spinae) by leaning forward in your chair and placing your chest on your thighs. Then press yourself into an upright position and pull your shoulders back (scapular retraction) to stretch your chest (pectorals). Stretch the sides of your trunk (obliques) by twisting slowly to one side and then the other. Rest your ankle on your thigh in a figure-4 position. Lean your chest toward your knee, stretching your hip (gluteus and piriformis). Switch legs and repeat.

Because your cardio kickboxing workout utilizes so many muscles, it's important to develop all-around flexibility. When you stretch, try and identify the places you feel tightest. Devote a little more time and attention to those areas. In addition, I recommend that you test the flexibility of your major kicking muscles. You'll spend a lot of time kicking during your workout, so it's important to have good flexibility in your legs.

To test your quadriceps, lie on your stomach. Bend one of your knees and see if your can bring your heel close to your hip. Switch legs and repeat. Good flexibility should allow you to do this.

To test your hamstrings, lie on your back. While keeping your left leg flat on the floor, raise your right leg as far toward your head as you can. Keep both knees almost completely straight (soft). If you can raise your leg ninety degrees you have good flexibility. Switch legs and repeat.

To test your hip flexors, lie on your back and grab your thigh behind your left knee. Keep your right leg flat on the floor. If you can bring your thigh to your chest while your right leg remains flat on the floor, your hip flexor flexibility is good. Switch sides and repeat.

Remember, even five minutes of daily stretching is beneficial. Take stretch breaks throughout your day (even on the days you're not training) and make stretching a habit. You don't have to be a Yoga master or develop complicated routines to enjoy the benefits of daily stretching.

Torso Maintenance: Your Abs and Lower Back

Your torso (your core) is the connection between your upper and lower limbs. A synergy between body parts provides stability for your training. A powerful core, especially the lower back and abdominals, allows you to punch and kick with less likelihood of injury. Acute back injuries occur from failing to stabilize your torso.

Stand up and put your hands on your waist. Move in any direction. You do not have to move far before you feel your abdominals brace your stances.

It's a good idea to improve the balance and strength in your trunk. Build your back and abdominal muscles from the inside out. Rather than just worrying about a "six pack," train your core for internal stability. A good way to improve your core is to train your abdominals with crunches. You can also practice flexing your abdominals during your normal, upright stances. Why? Because most of your activities are performed while standing. Electromyography studies demonstrated that your obliques (side of your stomach muscles) are active when you are in any stance.

While you do your crunches, pay attention to your spine. Contract your stabilizers to stay in neutral. Although neutral is best, it is difficult to maintain. Develop a strong midsection, but not at the expense of a painful back. Crunches performed with a flat back are effective, but return to neutral after each repetition to maintain functional stability.

Neutral simply means a slight curve in your lower back (see Figure 3-1). A neutral spine places the least amount of pressure on your disks, ligaments, and bones. Excessive arching and flattening of your back stresses your spinal disks. This can lead to nerve root irritation, degeneration of the vertebrae, and herniated disks. Chronic pain may be caused by gravity pulling you out of alignment while you are sitting or standing.

It takes practice and muscular endurance to stay in neutral. Try spending five minutes in neutral. Add two minutes a week until you can sit through your favorite sitcom in neutral. Practice your neutral spine while sitting, standing, and exercising. While reading, think about your posture. Adjust your spine into pelvic neutrality. Notice how healthy it feels to release unwanted tension.

Bend your index finger back until it feels uncomfortable. An x-ray won't show what is causing your pain. When you return your finger back to normal, it feels fine. Similarly, some postures make your back unhappy. When a random sampling of subjects had their spines x-rayed, some showed abnormalities and others did not. Amazingly, some of the folks with spondylolysis and spondylolisthesis were pain-free. Others, who complained of severe back pain, showed no sign of deformity.

Poor fitness leads to poor posture. The same is true concerning the relationship between your quadriceps and hamstrings. Your hamstrings should be at least sixty percent as strong as your quadriceps (thigh muscles). Tight hip flexors and hamstrings, combined with weak abdominals and a weak upper back, may be a prime cause for muscle imbalance, asymmetry, and pain.

Drop this book on the floor. Bend down to pick it up. You probably twisted in your chair and leaned over sideways from your waist. Unsupported flexion with a shearing diagonal force is unhealthy for the disks in your low back.

Your disks are collagen packets filled with water. You are taller in the morning because your disks are not compressed from hours of standing or sitting. If you wake up and proceed directly to your training, your inflated disks may protrude into your spinal nerve, causing pain. Therefore, perform your training after a thorough warm-up.

Does your back hurt when you walk from one stance to another? Walking loads and unloads your disks, like a massage. With most muscular problems, moving around helps to relieve pain. But more serious ailments could be aggravated while walking or moving. This may be due to a nerve impingement or herniated disk. In these cases, walking exacerbates pain because of nerve involvement. Pulsing and throbbing pain, or temperature disturbances may be a vascular issue. Be sure to see a physician if you experience chronic back pain.

Sit in a chair with your left leg on the floor and your right ankle crossed over your left knee in a figure-4 position. Slowly bring your chest toward your right knee. Do you feel pain? Try your other leg. Disk injuries, muscular imbalances, and lack of flexibility in the gluteals and piriformis (the muscle under your hip) can create sciatic nerve problems. Check with your doctor if you feel tingling or numbness radiating down your leg.

Stretches to Relieve Low Back Pain

1. Lie on your back and bring your knees to your chest in a fetal position. This stretches your erector spinae and quadratus laborum.
2. Lift one knee to your chest and grab it with your arms. Let your other leg remain on the floor. Switch legs and repeat. This stretches your hip flexors.
3. Lean sideways into a wall keeping your pelvis stable. Bend sideways, not forward. This may help if you have a disk that protrudes sideways.
4. Sit in your chair and slowly twist sideways. Maintain a neutral spine throughout. This may relieve pressure on your disks.
5. Lie on your stomach. Raise your right arm and your left leg and hold this position for five seconds. Then raise your left arm and right leg and hold. This exercise strengthens your erector spinae and quadratus laborum in your back.
6. Roll over onto your hands and knees. Lift your upper back and stretch so that you resemble a mad cat. Hold this stretch for three seconds.
7. Stand with your right hand against a wall. Grab the top of your left foot with your left hand. Bend your left knee until you feel a stretch in your left quadriceps. Switch legs and repeat.

Strength Training

Resistance training can improve your cardio kickboxing performance. While strength training (that is, lifting weights) is good, it's not the only way to get faster and stronger. Resistance tubing and calisthenics can overload your muscles to increase your strength and muscular endurance to enhance your cardio kickboxing skills.

Your pectoralis major, anterior deltoids, and triceps muscles are innervated during your punches. Bench presses and pushups can target these muscle groups to increase the force and power of your technique. But don't forget to train your biceps and lattisimus dorsi, as these muscle groups are essential for the eccentric contraction of your punches.

Your kicking force may be improved by training your quadriceps, hip flexors, hamstrings, and gluteals. The best exercises to target these muscle groups include leg extensions, leg curls, and squats.

Be careful to stretch after your strength training in order to maintain your flexibility.

Safety Reminders

Jab. Stabilize your torso. Retract your arm on the same trajectory and at the same speed as you extend it.

Hook. Keep a ninety-degree bend in your arm. Pivot on your front foot, then turn your hip and shoulder into your punch.

Uppercut. Keep your elbow bent at ninety degrees. Lift your body into your punch. Rock your hip for power.

Bob and Weave. Turn your feet in the direction of your body. Keep your abdominals tight. Your knees should stay aligned with your toes.

Knee Strike. Keep your back straight. Point your knee to your target.

Front Kick. Keep your back straight. Bend from your hip, then your knee. Retract your leg on the same trajectory as you extend it. Don't drop your chest toward your knee.

Roundhouse Kick. Keep your abdominals tight. Don't try to kick too high. Flex your hip before your extend your knee. Retract your leg on the same trajectory as you extend it. Keep your back straight.

Side Kick. Raise your foot to your knee to chamber your leg. Extend your foot straight to the target. Keep your toes sideways so your hips don't open up. Retract your leg at the same speed and on the same trajectory as you extend it.

General Safety Tips

1. Keep your posture in perfect alignment.
2. Alignment is more important than the height of your kicks.
3. Modify difficult movements to fit YOUR body type.
4. Punch and kick from both sides. Be balanced.
5. Do not hop on one leg over and over.
6. Choose moves that are appropriate to your fitness level.
7. Keep your knees in line with your toes.

8. Don't bring your heel to your hips when you throw a kick because this causes your back to arch.

9. Leaning forward on your techniques can contribute to shin splints.

10. Don't jog on your toes because this can cause tight achilles tendons and shortened calf muscles.

11. Don't attempt any high-intensity movements during your warm-up.

12. Protect all of your joints from torque. If you twist your lower body, be sure your knees are aligned over your toes. To do this, when you pivot, be sure to raise your heel off the floor and unload the weight from your pivot foot. Then turn on the ball of your foot at the same time you turn your leg. To unload your foot, become weightless by adding a light hop to your pivot.

Three Cardio Kickboxing Programs

Level 1 Program: Twenty Minutes

1. Warm up and stretch for four minutes. Include horse stance pulses, square stance pulses, and front stance pulses in your warm-up (see Chapter 4).
2. Perform the touch-step footwork from Chapter 8 for four minutes at a low heart rate (HR). Alternate punches, palm heel strikes, elbow strikes, and hooks as you move.
3. Get in a fighting stance and throw unilateral reverse punches for three minutes at a medium HR. Be sure to switch sides. Throw your punches with power and speed.
4. Throw unilateral defensive side kicks for three minutes at a high HR. Kick for a minute-and-a-half with each leg.
5. Throw jab, reverse punch, and hook combinations for two minutes at a medium-to-high HR. Throw your combos for one minute on each side.
6. Cool down and stretch for four minutes at a low HR. Use the special cooldown from Chapter 9.

Level 2 Program: Forty Minutes

1. Warm up and stretch for four minutes at a low heart rate (HR). Use the touch step footwork from Chapter 8 and throw a variety of easy punches and strikes.
2. Add in more footwork for four minutes at a medium HR. Include shuffles, steps, and push-slides. Alternate sides and repeat.
3. Throw kicking/punching combinations for four minutes at a high HR. Include side kicks and reverse punch combos. Practice for two minutes on each side.
4. Use a variety of blocks from Chapter 7 to avoid imaginary attacks. Train for four minutes at a medium HR. Be sure to include slipping a punch, ducking under, and bobbing and weaving.
5. Kick for four minutes at a medium HR. Alternate between knee strikes and front kicks. Work both legs for two minutes each.
6. Try stepping kicks for ten minutes at a high HR. Throw front, side, roundhouse, and swing kicks as you move up and down the floor. Alternate legs with each kick.

7. Model your class leader for three minutes at a medium HR.

8. Cool down and stretch for seven minutes at a low HR. Include the special cooldown from Chapter 9.

Level 3 Program: Sixty Minutes

1. Warm up and stretch for four minutes at a low heart rate (HR). Include walking stances. Move up and down the floor.

2. Throw jab, reverse punch, and hook combinations for four minutes at a medium HR. Alternate sides.

3. Practice kicking combinations for four minutes at a high HR. Use rear leg front kicks, rear leg roundhouse kicks, rear leg side kicks, and rear leg swing kicks.

4. Throw punch/kick combinations for four minutes at a high HR. Throw a front kick-jab combo and repeat on the other side. Then throw a reverse punch-side kick-reverse punch combo and repeat on the other side.

5. Shadowbox for four minutes at a medium HR.

6. Use the plyometric drills in Chapter 13 for ten minutes at a high HR.

7. Practice blocking for four minutes at a medium HR. Include overhead blocks, catching a kick, punching a kick, and blocking a punch-kick combination.

8. Use the self-defense combinations from Chapter 13 for four minutes at a medium HR. Include low kicks and elbow strikes.

9. Throw bilateral uppercuts with speed for one minute at a high HR.

10. Try Olympic cardio kickboxing from Chapter 13 for eleven minutes at a high HR. Go for three three-minute rounds of high intensity kicking and punching with one minute of active rest between each round.

11. Practice the dynamic flexibility exercises in Chapter 11 for five minutes at a medium HR. Include front, side, and roundhouse kicks.

12. Perform the wrist and shoulder alignment exercise from Chapter 13 for one minute. This is a low HR exercise. You can either do knuckle pushups or hold your body in the "up" position.

13. Cool down and stretch for four minutes at a low HR. Include the special cooldown from Chapter 9.

Interval Recovery Strategies

Use the following techniques during the recovery period of your interval workouts.

Overhead Block, Punch. Step forward with your left foot and throw a left overhead block. Follow up with a right reverse punch. Switch sides and repeat.

Downward Block, Punch. Step forward with your left foot and throw a left downward block. Follow up with a right reverse punch. Switch sides and repeat.

Stepping Double Punch. Step forward with your left foot and throw a left jab. Follow up with a right reverse punch. Switch sides and repeat.

Stepping Triple Punch. Step forward with your left foot and throw a left jab, a right reverse punch and another left jab. Switch sides and repeat.

Circular Hands. Begin in a fighting position with your left foot forward. Circle your hands as if you are blocking consecutive punches. Switch sides and repeat.

Light Bounce. Begin in a fighting position with your left foot forward. Bounce lightly on the balls of your feet and keep your hands up. Switch sides and repeat.

Switch Stances on the Downbeat. Begin in a fighting position with your left foot forward. Slowly switch to a right foot forward fighting position. Continue switching stances.

Moving Drill. Begin in a fighting position. Practice your shuffles, steps, shuffle-steps, and push-slides at a slow pace, then switch sides and repeat.

Bob and Weave. Begin in a fighting position with your left foot forward. Practice bobbing and weaving as you imagine an opponent throwing punches. Switch stances and repeat.

Relaxed Focus. Begin in a left foot forward fighting position. Imagine you are fighting an opponent and searching for an opening. Stay light on your feet in a guarded position. Switch stances often.

Marching Punch. While marching in place, throw slow punches to face level, chest level, and groin level.

Forward and Backward. While taking small steps forward, throw slow punches to face level, chest level, and groin level. When you reach one end of the room, step backwards while continuing to punch.

Jump Rope. Imagine that you are jumping rope very slowly.

Punch-Jacks. While doing a jumping-jack motion with your feet, throw simultaneous front punches when your legs are open. When your feet come together, retract your punches.

Shakedown. Begin standing in a ready position. With your arms to your sides, gently bounce up and down so that your feet barely leave the floor. Let your arms dangle at your sides and keep your neck relaxed.

Breathing Drill. Begin in a horse stance. Open your arms up to the sky as you take a deep cleansing breath from your diaphragm. As you exhale, let your arms to drop back down to your sides.

Interval Training with Effort Intervals and Active Rest

5 to 8 minutes	Warm up	
2 minutes	Stretch lightly	
30 seconds	Effort Interval	Rear leg front kick on the downbeat. Eight repetitions. Switch sides and repeat.
30 seconds	Active Recovery	Overhead block, reverse punch. Eight repetitions on the downbeat. Switch sides and repeat.
30 seconds	Effort Interval	Rear leg roundhouse kick. Eight repetitions on the downbeat. Switch sides and repeat.
30 seconds	Active Recovery	Downward block, reverse punch. Eight repetitions on the downbeat. Switch sides and repeat.

30 seconds	Effort Interval	Rear leg side kick. Eight repetitions on the downbeat. Switch sides and repeat.
30 seconds	Active Recovery	Stepping double punches. Eight repetitions on the downbeat. Switch sides and repeat.
30 seconds	Effort Interval	Rear leg side hook kick. Eight repetitions on the downbeat. Switch sides and repeat.
30 seconds	Active Recovery	Stepping triple punches. Eight repetitions on the downbeat. Switch sides and repeat.
30 seconds	Effort Interval	Rear leg swing kick Eight repetitions on the downbeat. Switch sides and repeat.

Cardio Kickboxing Q&A

Question: How do I improve my balance for cardio kickboxing?

Answer: Keep your supporting leg slightly bent on all of your kicks.

Question: How do I kick higher? My flexibility is not very good.

Answer: Practice the dynamic flexibility exercises in Chapter 11.

Question: What should I eat before training?

Answer: About an hour before your workout, eat some light carbohydrates.

Question: When will I begin to see results from my cardio kickboxing program?

Answer: Your energy level should increase almost immediately. Give yourself four weeks to notice other beneficial changes.

Question: Is cardio kickboxing a fad?

Answer: Only for those who quit the program. For many, it is a long-term lifestyle change.

Exercises to Avoid for At-Risk Populations—Older Adults, and Level 1 Cardio Kickboxers

- Back kicks
- Spin kicks
- Jump kicks
- Double kicks
- Plyometric drills
- High kicks
- Fast kicks
- Fast punches
- Highly choreographed drills
- Arousal-inducing strategies

Striking Surfaces

Kicks

Front kick: ball of the foot, heel, top of the foot, and point of your shoe.

Roundhouse kick: ball of the foot, top of the foot, and point of your shoe.

Side kick: knife edge (outside edge) of your foot and your heel.

Swing kick: knife edge (outside edge) of your foot and your heel.

Hand Techniques

All punches and the backfist strike: first two knuckles.

Knife hand strike: outside edge of your hand between your wrist and your little finger.

Palm heel strike: base of your palm just above your wrist and adjacent to your thumb.

Ridge hand strike: base of the knuckle of your index finger on the medial side of your hand (opposite of the knife hand).

Blocks

Overhead block: outside of your forearm.

Center block: inside of your forearm.

Downward block: outside of your forearm.

Inward block: outside of your forearm.

Ten Imagery Cues to Improve Your Motivation

1. Imagine you are being attacked. Throw a front leg side kick to stop your attacker, and a front hand hook to finish him off.

2. Visualize that you are evading an opponent. Practice moving forward, backward, and side to side.

3. Picture an attacker trying to punch you in the head. Duck under and counterattack with a rear hand reverse punch.

4. While maintaining a fighting stance, imagine you are as relaxed as a dishrag, without tension. And then explode with a lightning fast defensive reverse punch to stop your imaginary opponent.

5. Get a mental picture of yourself throwing a jab, reverse punch, and hook combination. Feel the energy traveling from your brain to your muscles. Immediately deliver this three-punch combination with perfect form.

6. To increase your speed, mentally rehearse that there is NO TIME between the initiation of your jab and its completion. The start is simultaneous with the finish—pure speed.

7. As your imaginary opponent attacks your head with a punch, immediately counter with an overhead block and reverse punch combination.

8. To quicken your shuffle, visualize your front foot "pulling" your back foot into a position to replace it.

9. To improve your flexibility, breathe into your muscles, and imagine your muscle fibers lengthening with each stretch.

10. To relax during your cooldown, simply focus on your breath. If any thoughts other than your breath enter your mind, let them go in one ear and out the other and go back to your breath.

A Word About Heart Rate Monitors

A new trend is to use heart rate (HR) monitors during your cardio kickboxing. I am not a proponent of using HR monitors during cardio kickboxing. The formulas to predict maximum HR are not accurate in most cases. There is a twelve to fifteen beat-per-minute (either high or low) error when using HR prediction formulas. Therefore, they are too imprecise for "zone training" in cardio kickboxing.

As we discussed in Chapter 9, even when maximum HR is procured by a graded exercise test or a field test, different individuals respond differently to a given percentage of their maximum HR.

Also, maximum achievable HRs tend to be different in various activities. Maximum HR is lower on a bike than running or cardio kickboxing. So a training HR that is used during group indoor cycling may not be appropriate during cardio kickboxing.

Finally, HR response to exercise is affected by variables including medications, hydration levels, overtraining, and illness. It is critically important to listen to your body, with or without a HR monitor.

Muscles Used in Cardio Kickboxing Techniques

Jab. Your shoulder flexes, beginning your movement. To do this, your anterior deltoid and medial deltoid are innervated. Your triceps brachii extend your elbow to complete your jab.

Reverse Punch. Your spine rotates when your internal and external obliques contract to begin your body motion. Then, just as in your jab, your anterior and medial deltoid contract. Finally, your triceps brachii complete the reverse punch.

Hook. Your internal and external obliques begin the movement in your upper body. Then your pectoralis major (chest) and anterior deltoid contract simultaneously. Your serratus, anterior, and medial deltoid remain contracted as you complete your hook.

Uppercut. Your internal and external obliques begin the movement in your upper body. Then your medial and anterior deltoid contract as your elbow remains flexed to complete your uppercut.

Front Kick. Your iliopsoas (hip flexor) and rectus femoris raise your knee into a fold position. Then your quadriceps contract to extend your knee. Your hamstrings stop your contraction and actually help to pull your extended foot back into a flexed knee position. Finally, your iliopsoas and rectus femoris contract eccentrically to return your foot to its original position.

Roundhouse Kick. Your fist movement is hip abduction. This concentric contraction involves your gluteus medius and tensor fasciae latae. Simultaneously, your iliopsoas and rectus femoris contract. Just as in your front kick, your quadriceps are responsible for knee extension. At the completion of your kick, your hamstrings contract eccentrically to stop your knee from hyperextending. Your hamstrings are also involved in retracting your foot back into your fold position. At the same time, your hip adducts eccentrically and your iliopsoas and rectus femoris also eccentrically contract to return your foot to its original position.

Side Kick. Your side kick begins by concentrically contracting your iliopsoas (hip flexor) and rectus femoris to bring your foot to the fold position. Then, your tensor faciae latae and gluteus medius are responsible for abducting your hip. Your quadriceps extend your knee to complete your side kick. Then your gluteus medius and tensor fasciae latae eccentrically contract to adduct your hip. And at the same time, your quadriceps return your foot to its original position by extending your knee back to the floor.

SUGGESTED READING

Anderson, B. *Stretching,* Shelter Publications, 1980.

Benson, H. *Beyond the Relaxation Response,* Times Books, 1984.

Benson, H. *Your Maximum Mind,* Times Books, 1987.

Benson, H. *The Wellness Book,* Simon & Schuster, 1993.

Borysenko, J. *Minding the Body, Mending the Mind,* Bantam Books, 1988.

Csikszentmihalyi, M. *Flow: The Psychology of Optimal Experience,* Simon & Schuster, 1994.

Dossey, L. *Healing Words,* Harper Collins, 1993.

Edwards, S. *The Heart Rate Monitor Book,* Polar Electro, 1993.

Goleman, D. *Mind Body Medicine,* Consumer Reports Books, 1993.

Langer, E. *Mindfulness,* Addison Wesley, 1989.

Seabourne, T. *The Martial Arts Athlete—Mental and Physical Conditioning for Peak Performance,* YMAA Publication Center, 1998.

Seabourne, T. *Power Body—Injury Prevention, Rehabilitation, and Sport Performance Enhancement,* YMAA Publication Center, 1999.

About the Author

Tom Seabourne, Ph.D., is a sport psychologist, two-time National AAU Taekwondo champion, and a silver medalist in the World Taekwondo Championships. He is also an ESPN Professional Karate Association full-contact karate champion.

He is a certified strength and conditioning specialist (CSCS), and holds certifications with the American Council on Exercise (ACE) and the American College of Sports Medicine (ACSM).

Tom has authored over two hundred articles on fitness and sports psychology, and is the author of seven books, including *The Martial Arts Athlete—Mental and Physical Conditioning for Peak Performance* and *Power Body—Injury Prevention, Rehabilitation, and Sport Performance Enhancement*, both available from YMAA Publication Center (www.ymaa.com).

Tom writes a weekly fitness column in the Longview News Journal in Texas entitled "Your Personal Trainer." He also hosts a weekly radio call-in show called "Total Fitness."

In addition to his martial arts and fitness training, Tom is an avid cyclist. He is a winner of the RAAM Open West, and placed in the top ten in the Race Across America. He holds two Texas state cycling records, as well as Arkansas and Louisiana state cycling records. He is a national 12-hour cycling record holder and the 1995 24-hour Texas state cycling champion.

Tom has been featured in *Sports Illustrated* magazine three times, including *Sports Illustrated's* Athlete of the Month.

Tom maintains a fitness website at www.onlinetofitness.com.

Resource Page

Sport Karate, Inc.
Cardio Kickboxing® instructor certification program
17 Foreside Road, Cumberland Foreside, ME 04110
1-800-270-KICK (5425)
email: cardiokick@wowpages.com
www.wowpages.com/cardiokick

Kickbox Fitness
Cardio Kickboxing®
Joe Lewis' Kickbox Fitness certification
877-333-5269 (toll free)
www.kickboxfitness.com

Exercise Etc.
Cardio Kickboxing®
800-244-1344

Sara City Workout
Cardio Kickboxing®
800 545-CITY

Topper Sportsmedicine
Cardio Kickboxing® products
800-555-3001

L.A. Fitness
Cardio Kickboxing®
800-600-2540

ECA World Fitness
Cardio Kickboxing®
800-ECA-3976

Century
Cardio Kickboxing® products
800-626-2787

Universal
Cardio Kickboxing® nutrition
800-USA-0101

Index

Books & Videos from YMAA

YMAA Publication Center Books

YMAA Publication Center Videotapes

YMAA Publication Center    楊氏東方文化出版中心

4354 Washington Street Roslindale, MA 02131
1-800-669-8892 • ymaa@aol.com • www.ymaa.com